MENCIUS AND MASCULINITIES

SUNY series in Chinese Philosophy and Culture

Roger T. Ames, editor

MENCIUS AND MASCULINITIES

Dynamics of Power, Morality, and Maternal Thinking

Joanne D. Birdwhistell

STATE UNIVERSITY OF NEW YORK PRESS

Published by
State University of New York Press
Albany

Printed in the United States of America

For information, address
State University of New York Press
Albany, NY
www.sunypress.edu

Production, Michael Haggett
Marketing, Anne M. Valentine

Library of Congress Cataloging-in-Publication Data

Birdwhistell, Joanne D., 1944-
Mencius and masculinities : dynamics of power, morality, and maternal thinking / Joanne D. Birdwhistell.
p. cm — (SUNY series in Chinese philosophy and culture)
Includes bibliographical references and index.
ISBN-13: 978-0-7914-7029-9 (hardcover : alk. paper)
ISBN-13: 978-0-7914-7030-5 (pbk. : alk. paper)
1. Mencius. 2. Philosophy, Chinese—To 221 B.C. 3. Gender identity in literature. I. Title.
B128.M324B57 2007
181'.112—dc22 2006025043

10 9 8 7 6 5 4 3 2 1

In memory of my mother and my father

and for my sisters Claire and Jamie

and our next generation, Carrie, Julie, Winona, Melina, and Zachary

Contents

Acknowledgments

This work represents my efforts to bring together two separate fields of knowledge in which I have long been interested—Chinese philosophy and feminist theory. I studied Chinese philosophy during both my undergraduate and graduate years. My experiences while teaching at The Richard Stockton College of New Jersey led me into additional areas, beyond my earlier grounding in Asian studies. I thank my Stockton colleagues, especially Rodger Jackson and Anne Pomeroy, and my students for their encouragement of my intellectual journeys.

Although most of the views and arguments of this study were worked out in my classes at Stockton, two papers that I presented discussed earlier versions of some of these ideas. I thank Bruce Brooks and his associates for the opportunity to present my paper, "The Maternal in *Mencius*," at the Warring States Conference, University of Massachusetts, Amherst, MA, October 13–14, 2000. I also thank Columbia University for the opportunity to present my paper, "Gender Matters in *Mencius*: The Hidden? Dimension of Maternal Teachings in Confucian Thought," at the Neo-Confucian Regional Seminar, Columbia University, New York, NY, November 3, 2000. In addition, I am indebted to Stockton College for having provided me with a sabbatical during which I was able to begin this study full time. I have learned much from my colleagues and friends in the fields of Chinese studies and Western philosophy, and I thank them all for their ideas and their efforts to promote a global conversation in philosophy. Finally, I wish to thank Roger T. Ames for his leadership in the field of comparative philosophy and the two readers who reviewed my manuscript for SUNY Press and offered helpful suggestions and comments. I take full responsibility, however, for the interpretations that I offer here.

Introduction

It is well known that philosophers disagree on a number of issues, including the very nature of philosophical ideas themselves. Two of the many questions that concern this issue are whether gender is a critical dimension of philosophical ideas and whether the original historical context of an idea is a critical aspect of that idea. A negative answer to both of these questions suggests a belief that philosophical ideas are somehow abstract or universal, while a positive answer implies the converse, namely, that ideas are specific or particular. Taking the latter position in this study of *Mencius*, I analyze how gender functions as a critical dimension of the philosophical ideas in this important Chinese text.

This study involves several aims. The first is to make a claim about the particularity of philosophical ideas and to support that claim by means of a close analysis of the text of *Mencius*. My second aim is to illustrate that, and how, gender is one aspect of such particularity. In other words, I maintain that, despite their apparent universality, philosophical concepts are particular in their applications. This is due to the fact that in the process of abstraction and generalization many specific characteristics of the original social-historical context are lost. What remains as a philosophical idea are only those traits important to the perspective of the privileged position. Other traits may be important to other positions, those who have no voice, but they are lost as the ideas become generalized. Philosophical ideas thus reflect particular, not universal, perspectives, and gender remains as one of those particular traits whether it is attended to or not in the formation of concepts.

My third aim, which is the focus of this study, is to demonstrate how Mencian ideas concerning the great man, the gentlemen, or the benevolent ruler involve cultural processes of appropriation, transformation, and transcoding. Maternal practices and thinking are, in effect, appropriated and transformed into filial practices, which are in turn transformed into those advocated for the benevolent ruler, who is to be "father and mother of the people." Since the text refers explicitly and often to agricultural practices while remaining silent on matters of maternal thought and practices, the transcoding of maternal and agricultural thought enables the maternal context to serve as an unacknowledged theoretical dimension of Mencian moral thinking.

A final aim is to apply to a Chinese philosophical text a method of textual analysis I first learned from Western feminist theorists, who have examined the ideas of many Western philosophers from a gender viewpoint. Although I have learned various approaches to methodology from feminist theorists, the analyses and interpretations presented here are my own.

Chapter 1 takes up a range of theoretical concerns that arise from reading texts in nontraditional ways, or, against the grain. Maintaining that Chinese philosophy was historically a discourse about competing forms of masculinity, I discuss how female gendered behavior nonetheless had a central role in the dynamics of Mencian thinking. At the same time, it would be a mistake to assume that women themselves were viewed as a subject of extended concern or in a fully favorable way. Still, while their interests were not the topic of Mencian thought, they generally supported Mencian moral ideas. I also note the historical importance of *Mencius* (*Mengzi* 孟子) and the fact that, like all the primary philosophical texts, it has been the subject of various commentaries. Indeed, Chinese philosophers often presented their ideas in the form of commentaries on classical texts, thus offering interpretations that reflected their differing historical concerns. In a somewhat comparable way, my position in this study is to analyze *Mencius* from the viewpoint of a contemporary issue, that of gender, although I do consider its ideas to be inseparable from their historical context.

Chapter 2 consists of an explanation of my methodological approach and theoretical assumptions. I begin with the assumption that, by conceiving texts as cultural landscapes, we can turn our attention to any of their aspects rather than only to what the authors focus on. While gender is neither a topic of discussion in *Mencius* nor a concern of previous commentaries, many references to gender occur in the text. Thus, I first address the various ways in which gender is communicated. The second part of chapter 2 clarifies my approach to philosophical ideas in terms of social practices, contexts, and human relations, all of which serve to remind us of the embodied nature of ideas. I examine characteristics both of maternal practices and thinking and of farming practices and thinking. My thesis is that Mencian ideas about masculinity are derived in a fundamental, but unacknowledged, way from maternal experience, and the Mencian concept of the heart is a central marker of this linkage. Since the farming and maternal contexts are transcoded, the explicit discussions of issues relating to farming elicit ideas about maternal practices, which are not discussed in the text.

Although the first two chapters address aspects of the issue of gender, I have a few preliminary comments on the topic. In brief, in the ancient world of China (and elsewhere), distinctions between sex and gender were not typically made. Thus, male, man, and masculine were interchangeable notions. What a man did and the contexts of his actions were male or masculine. As the text indicates in many ways, Mencius was speaking to men, about men, and about men's activities and actions. The issue for him was the kinds of behavior that should be included in the range of desirable male/masculine actions. Mencius was promoting a kind of behavior that he felt would best achieve the aims and values of his thinking, and he argued for his model of behavior in various ways, including an appeal to certain historical sage figures and pragmatic reasoning. He did not claim that he was inventing any kind of new behavior.

Although Mencius was not speaking about women's/female/feminine behavior, he was concerned to show that the male behavior he advocated was not the same as women's behavior—it was not feminine, even though some people might have (wrongly) thought so. Specific actions of men, however much they might physically or visually resemble those of women, were not feminine because a man's actions were done, and judged, in reference to a certain type of context, namely, a male sphere of action and expectations. The cultural interpretation of behavior was a matter of social relations and contexts. In other words, the concept of gender refers to the social-cultural meaning of an act (or of behavior), or said slightly differently, it refers to the communication of social-cultural meaning by means of behavior. Gender is not a concept that operates on a physical or muscular level. It operates on a cultural level in a cultural and communicational context.

To cite an example from *Mencius*, a man's picking up a baby at the edge of a well is a different act, from the perspective of gender, from a woman's picking up a baby at the edge of a well. The physical act may be the same but the gendered meaning is different. A man's performance of certain actions that Mencius labeled compassionate was not feminine behavior because his actions were done in reference to a male sphere of activity and its relevant standards for judging success. His actions meant that he was cultivating the way of the sages. Mencius rejected attempts to associate, prematurely and without reference to social context, particular actions of men with actions of women because he assumed that the context or social setting was an important part of the behavior.

An example from *Zhuangzi* 莊子, a Daoist text of the same period as *Mencius*, further illustrates the contextual dimension of ideas. The gourd master's action of staying home and cooking the family's meals was not feminine behavior because it was done in reference to his cultivation of the *dao* 道 (way) and his rejection of the norms of society for men. His act of cooking meals meant that he was living in a free and sagely way and had successfully rejected society's duties and restrictions. The meaning of his wife's cooking was very different, however. It was her social duty to do so. Her cooking implied that she was fulfilling her social duties, and so for her, cooking was feminine.

Chapters 3 and 4 respectively present detailed analyses of Mencius' arguments against two rejected models of masculine behavior, which I term the agrarian masculinity of Shen Nong and the self-centered masculinity of King Hui. The agrarian type of masculinity is best illustrated in passage 3A4, in which we see how this model of male behavior blurs social and class distinctions and focuses on the small matters of everyday life, rather than the large matters of government. Chapter 3 is restricted to a close gender analysis of 3A4 in its entirety. In addressing the self-centered model of male behavior in chapter 4, I broaden the discussion to include important related assumptions. One such assumption concerns the relational nature of personal identities, while another is the view that the conceptions of those forming a relational pair are inseparable from the characteristics of their interaction. Thus, a change in the conceptions of the ruler and of the people also entails a change in their behavior toward each other. Passages scattered throughout the text contain Mencius' criticisms of the self-centered type of masculinity, which he considers inhumane and dismissive of personal family relations. It should be stressed, however, that both of these models of masculinity have some characteristics that Mencius admires and some he rejects.

Chapters 5, 6, and 7 discuss Mencius' ideas about a benevolent government, with chapter 5 focusing on the topic of governmental practices and chapters 6 and 7 addressing the development of the ruler as a person. Chapter 5 delves into the economic, educational, and political measures of compassionate governing and indicates how the dynamics of the practices of compassionate governing compare with those of maternal practices. In identifying the terms used to refer to such a government and in describing its policies and practices, this chapter brings out ways in which Mencius makes the governing context analogous to the familial context. A number of characteristics link the two contexts together, with an important one being feelings. These include, among others, joy, affection, and compassion. The actions associated with such feelings point to a transformation of certain maternal and familial practices into masculine, governmental, and patriarchal practices.

Chapters 6 and 7 focus on the Mencian ideal of masculinity as it is embodied in the ruler as a person. The ruler must develop himself morally in two contexts, that of his own family and that of the state or empire, and he does so by cultivating himself in the situations that apply to him from among the five relations. His behavior is important because he serves as a model for action both within the family and the empire. By embodying the ideal Mencian behavior in specific contexts and relations, the ruler can not only teach people what to do, he can also motivate them to put these ideas into actual practice.

Chapter 6 discusses the ruler's development of himself in the relations of father and son and of older brother and younger brother, while pointing out that Mencius' emphasis is on the adult son and younger brother in positions of responsibility. The position of son is most critical, moreover, for it functions within, and links together, the patriarchal relation of father and son and the maternal context of mother and son. Through the association of concepts of moral behavior, practices of the state and of the family become transcoded. That is, by his own cultivation of Mencian moral behavior as it applies to sons and younger brothers, the ruler initiates a process in which governmental relations become transformed into family relations. By copying the ruler's example, the people learn to behave as exemplary sons and younger brothers within their families and the empire.

Chapter 7 analyses the further transformations that lead to the development of a truly benevolent ruler, whom Mencius calls father and mother of the people. The process of transformation entails the ruler's incorporating certain maternal practices into his behavior and so eliciting a new kind of behavior from the people. That is, within the family the ruler becomes a filial son to his father by embodying certain practices of maternal compassion learned from his mother. When he extends this new kind of male behavior toward the people within the context of the empire, he becomes father and mother of the people and they become like children, or perhaps even like responsible adult sons. As a result of the ruler's embodying the new Mencian form of masculinity and the people's responding in kind, political relations within the empire become analogous to those within the family.

Chapter 8, the culminating section theoretically, analyzes from the viewpoint of gender Mencian ideas about the heart, or heart-mind, and the feelings and actions thought to spring spontaneously from the heart. Here I offer the view that compassion was originally the pivotal feeling among the four feelings and that a naturally compassionate heart, or a heart unable to endure others' suffering, was originally attributed only to women, especially to women as mothers. In advocating a type of male behavior that opposed cruelty and included practices that some considered maternal or feminine, Mencius was thus making a then radical claim that "all men [too] have this [maternal] heart [of compassion]." Chapter 8 also discusses such topics as the role of courage in Mencius' thinking, the ways that Mencius blunts the issue of shame by distancing this form of masculinity from women's behavior, and the feelings of pleasure that sagely behavior brings.

Concluding this study with chapter 9, I offer a very brief summary of the theoretical position presented here and return to the issue of why it is important to recognize that Mencian concepts of morality have a gender dimension. Such recognition is relevant both to the search for knowledge and to political and social change in the contemporary world. We must not allow the two to become separated.

Chapter 1

Hidden in Plain View

Questions, Issues, and Perspectives

We can read a text in many ways, and what we find depends in great part on the questions we bring to our reading. The richness in texts and approaches enables us as contemporary readers gain a better understanding of the complexities of the thought and world of the ancient philosophers. While the text of Mencius has been the subject of numerous studies, contemporary developments in scholarship invite its further examination. These developments are of various kinds, with some the result of recent archeological discoveries, while others related to a greater awareness of the assumptions that shape our investigations.

Inspired by the latter kind of advance, I offer here an examination of Mencian thought and argumentation from the perspective of gender.[1] Studies of *Mencius* to date have generally not been concerned with gender or have seen the Mencian position as largely favorable to women because of its inclusion of values typically associated with women. Both approaches have thus assumed, whether implicitly or explicitly, that Mencian moral and political concepts were gender neutral, theoretically applying to both men and women. I claim here that such gender neutrality was not the case and that Mencian teachings applied specifically to men, especially those in privileged positions. In addition, gender was not an extraneous component of Mencian moral and political concepts. It was embedded in philosophical discourse at all levels, from the assumptions and words themselves, to the content and contexts of argumentation.

Recognizing the gender specificity of Mencian ideas is important because it affects our interpretation of central Mencian claims. If we read through a gender lens, we will be able to understand the behavioral dynamics of how a man was to become a great man (*daren* 大人), the Mencian ideal of the moral person, and how the process related to cultural understandings of men and women. By not attending to the gender dimension of Mencius' views, we miss both how radical and conservative his position was, and we forego gaining certain insights into the Confucian-Mencian tradition and its relation to Chinese society and culture.

I begin this study with several observations, which will be supported here briefly and more extensively in the course of the following discussion. First, viewed in terms of gender, Chinese philosophy is a story about competing forms of masculinity. Recorded in texts dating from the earliest times to the present, philosophical conflicts and activities have been carried out primarily in reference to the male sphere of society and government. The thinkers, ideas, texts, and actions belonged to a masculine realm of political power and culture from ancient to contemporary China. As an ongoing conversation on how to behave, Chinese philosophy was an affair of elite men, for they were the ones who both developed the ideas and established the perspectives for their understanding. Their concerns, not those of women and nonelite men, filled the pages of the texts. Nonetheless, women and their behavior were relevant to the philosophical conversation.

A second observation is that various kinds of forgetting have occurred within the Chinese philosophical tradition. The most obvious kind is that revealed by recent archeological discoveries, which have brought to light ancient texts and ideas lost for two millennia.[2] Another type of forgetting has happened with the burying of ideas in the received texts themselves. That is, some ideas were embedded but remained unrecognized in the known texts, contained subversively in the texture of the texts' explicit arguments. While certainly elusive, suppressed arguments appearing in fragmented form within the texts have kept open the possibility for some of the forgotten ideas to re-emerge. Such fragments hint at the existence of issues or conflicts whose losers had to record their ideas, and perhaps even the conflicts, elsewhere, in sites other than the philosophical texts. Although details have long been lost, cultural memories remain, transformed and transmitted in narratives, images, symbols, and words.

By reconstructing parts of these forgotten conversations, we can see how Mencius argued for his views. His arguments were fraught with potential difficulties, of course, for they entailed the inclusion of values derived from female gendered behavior while excluding actual women. An early pre-Mencius textual illustration of the process of exclusion occurs, for instance, in the response of Confucius (Kongzi 孔子, 551 BCE–479 BCE) to King Wu's comment about having ten capable officials. Half a millennium after King Wu, a founder of the Zhou dynasty (1027? BCE–

256 BCE), Confucius said that there were only nine, for one was a woman.[3] In other words, serving as an official was male gendered behavior, even if one was an actual woman.

Told in many cultural forms, not only in texts, the philosophical argument that I reconstruct here is about how female gendered behavior was central to Confucian-Mencian thinking, even as the teachings concerned the actions of men. My thesis is not that women were central in the sense of *yinyang* 陰陽 thinking, however, which offers the framework of an all-encompassing and complementary binary system. Rather, women were central in a more fundamental, nonbinary, and pre-*yinyang* sense, in which women embodied the seemingly unknowable and indestructible creative source of life.[4] My account concerns how Mencian thinking appropriated fundamental characteristics of women as mothers and wives and, through certain processes of transformation, applied these characteristics to elite men in their social-political realms, thereby constructing philosophical concepts and views.[5] Such processes of appropriation and transformation remained characteristic of this classical tradition as it developed over time, although specific cultural and ideological meanings of these processes changed with the contexts. Current scholarship suggests, moreover, that such gendering processes are continuing in the present, well beyond the boundaries of the former Confucian (*ru* 儒) or classical imperial order.[6]

The textual range of my analysis is intentionally limited, for it is the particulars in the claims and argumentation that reveal how ideas and concepts mean certain kinds of behavior. To provide a sufficiently detailed analysis of the processes by which female gendered behavior helps construct Confucian-Mencian thinking, I offer a close reading only of *Mencius*, a text of the Warring States period (480 BCE–221 BCE) and one of the most important works in the tradition. My focus concerns Mencian argumentation and the sociopsychological processes that enable a man to become a great man, or a gentleman (*junzi* 君子).[7]

Mencius is especially appropriate to analyze from a gender viewpoint because of its contributions to Confucian thought and its philosophical importance both historically and in our contemporary world. Although Confucian and Mencian views were widely challenged when first advocated, they eventually became critical to the moral, social, and political foundation of the Chinese imperial order, which lasted well into the nineteenth century. Mencius was the first major follower of Confucius in the received tradition, and the text that bears his name became especially important from the Song period (960–1279) on.[8] During the Song it was accorded classical status by Zhu Xi 朱熹 (1130–1200) as one of the Four Books, along with the Confucian *Analects* (*Lunyu* 論語), *Great Learning* (*Daxue* 大學), and *Focusing the Familiar* or *The Mean* (*Zhongyong* 中庸). The Four Books together with Zhu Xi's commentaries formed the basis of the civil service examination system in the early fourteenth century, and this educational-political system remained in effect until 1905. Contemporary adherents and sympathizers of New Confucianism continue to place special value on *Mencius*, and scholars remain very much interested in it.[9]

Viewed historically, it has been (and continues to be) a text of constantly changing meanings, for thinkers have successively interpreted it in light of their own particular concerns and cultural circumstances.[10] Although my reading is from a perspective of contemporary interest, I still treat *Mencius* as a text from a particular historical period. I consider its ideas to be based on specific assumptions and issues of its time, even though we know only some of the historical particulars now. I also maintain that we do not need to, and must not, decontextualize *Mencius* from its historical setting in order to make it relevant today, since many ancient issues continue to be important. The *Mencius* I discuss is not the one that Song thinkers understood from their political and ontological perspectives, or that Qing (1644–1911) thinkers understood with their concerns of evidential research, or that some contemporary thinkers understand in terms of Enlightenment-based assumptions. I address a dimension of Mencian thinking that was of no explicit interest to the thinkers and writers of traditional Chinese or Western philosophy but still pervades the text.

In addition to the history of the changes in understanding this text, there is another kind of story involving *Mencius*, namely the compilation of the text itself during the Warring States period. From the work of textual dating and compilation of E. Bruce Brooks and A. Taeko Brooks, we know that *Mencius* like many texts was compiled over a period of time. The compilation of this text continued beyond the life of Mencius himself, who died about 303 BCE.[11] According to the Brooks' analysis, the text consists of a number of layers, which they identify with a Northern and a Southern school. They date the original interviews of Mencius to ca. 320–310 BCE, with additional material being added in various ways until 249 BCE, when Lu ceased to exist as a state and further textual activity also stopped.

The history of this text is relevant to many scholarly questions including a few of my concerns here, but it is outside the primary aims of my analysis. Moreover, since much of the text consists of statements not made by Mencius himself but still attributed to him, I have taken the liberty of referring to all of the ideas as if they were actually stated by Mencius, in order to avoid numerous clumsy phrases and circumlocutions. We need to keep in mind, however, that when we examine this text from the perspective of the history of its compilation, we see a clear development in ideas. Thus, when this development is relevant to my analysis, I indicate whether a passage is from an earlier or later layer of the text.

My discussion is mostly based on what can be found within the text itself, although information from other writings helps suggest the philosophical significance of my claims. Some data illustrate, for instance, how maternal relations and female gendered behavior were historically central to Confucian-Mencian thinking. Not addressed directly as an issue and not a topic of teaching in the classical philosophical works, maternal practices are mentioned occasionally in texts in regard to other ideas, and mothers themselves were clearly recognized as important throughout Chinese society in both earlier and later periods. In the *Odes* (*Shijing* 詩經), for instance, the mother of the ancient sage ruler King Wen, a founder of the Zhou dynasty along with his son King Wu, was admired for teaching her son the proper virtues.[12] The mothers or maternal families of Confucius and Mencius were seen as critical to their early education and upbringing. Both thinkers were thought of as orphans, and both experienced a distancing from the paternal family.[13] Later on, other philosophers in the tradition, the famous and not so famous, such as Zhu Xi and Li Yong 李顒 (1627–1705) respectively, were also depicted as orphans, that is, fatherless, even though they were not young children when their fathers died.[14] There was, in other words, an ongoing cultural message that mothers are especially important for a man's success.

Some texts, such as the *Biographies of Exemplary Women* (*Lienüzhuan* 列女傳) from the Han period (206 BCE–220 CE), relate the importance of mothers both within and beyond the Confucian tradition. Called the way of mother and son (*muzizhidao* 母子之道), the mother and son relationship from the later Han to late imperial times was recognized as having great significance among the political elite.[15] By the seventeenth and eighteenth centuries, and possibly much earlier, women's lives and the women's quarters were openly viewed as the position of genuine morality and as the moral center of society. Considered outside the political sphere of elite men with its turbulence and corruption, women's practices and places (the home) were seen as tangible embodiments of supposedly unchanging Confucian moral values.[16]

Such information suggests the existence of ongoing gender issues implicitly embedded within Confucian-Mencian discourse but not addressed openly. Despite its personal, social, and philosophical importance from the classical to the late imperial period, the mother and son relationship was not one of the five recognized Confucian relations. It did not belong to the Confucian-Mencian theoretical social ontology, which for centuries characterized the social order in terms of the five relations (*renlun* 人倫) and four classes (*simin* 四民). The only relation among the five involving actual women was that of husband and wife. This relation was a theoretically recognized male relation, in contrast to that of mother and son, which was not. In other words, this social ontology described a world that was patriarchal, hierarchical, based on family and patrilineage, and fundamentally gendered. This ontology rendered women largely invisible in the philosophical texts, insofar as it applied to male relations and the texts did not address women's relationships, as it did those of men.

The theoretical exclusion of the mother and son relationship from this ontology is confirmed in many ways, both obvious and subtle. One way consists of the explicit references to the father and son relation throughout the *Analects* and *Mencius* (and other texts, such as *Xunzi* 荀子), while simply not mentioning women's relationships. We also find that when different kinds of behavior are ranked in a moral sense, the examples focus on men and behavior that is socially and politically applicable to them.[17] A further method of exclusion is the typical reference to men in terms of rank and occupation and to women in terms of their sex or marital status.[18] All four of these characterizations (rank, occupation, sex, and marital status) are social-political in a contemporary sense, but only the former two are of philosophical concern within the Confucian-Mencian ontology.

While gender can be defined in various ways, here it refers to certain forms of patterned behavior within a cultural and communicational system. Evident in the earliest records in China, gender is culturally encoded in a variety of forms. It pertains not only to a person's positions and behavior in the family, state, and economic realms, but also to the more personal dimensions of one's body movements and appearance, and one's aims, expectations, and hopes in life. How gender has been thought about and its cultural meanings have changed over time.[19] Although gender has been an aspect of *yinyang* correlative and metonymic thinking throughout most of Chinese history, *Mencius* was compiled prior to the extensive development of *yinyang* theory, a phenomenon of the Han period. Before the full acceptance of *yinyang* theory, texts tended to describe personal behavior in terms of particular social situations or practices of women and men, rather than categorize it in terms of abstract cosmic patterns linked to *yinyang* polarities.

The move from a particular to a more abstract level of thinking about behavior did not, however, obliterate previous forms of masculine gender fluidity, a significant characteristic linking earlier and later periods. The great male heroes of the early Zhou dynasty, men such as Kings Wen and Wu and the slightly later Zhong Shanfu, are described in the *Odes*, for instance, in terms of both masculine and feminine traits. *Tian* 天 (an important religious and philosophical term with a range of meanings and so variously translated as Heaven, conditions, circumstances, and forces) is similarly depicted; it is associated with the male and with force, and yet it also gives birth.[20]

Although such transgendering may appear to be favorable to women by the valuing of feminine traits, such a conclusion is deceptive, for the processes of appropriation and transformation entail silencing. Mencius' moral ideal may have been androgynous, but he remained a male. The concept of androgyny itself is problematic, moreover, because it implicitly affirms a binary sex and gender system, and it supports certain cultural values derived from binary patterns of the cosmos. Thus, in examining Mencian ideas about masculinities, it is helpful to consider such questions as where women are situated socially, whether the great women who also appear in the *Odes* and other ancient texts are comparably masculine and feminine, and what the philosophical implications are of the elite male's incorporating some but not all gender traits of women.

At the same time that the early Confucian-Mencian thinkers were promoting an implicitly transgendered ideal, elite men were strongly discouraged from exhibiting certain types of feminine behavior.[21] This phenomenon suggests that, by the time of philosophical textual development, a selectivity of vision was prevalent with regard to the recognition of gendered behavior. That is, some behavior that had originally been appropriated from women was generally not recognized as such and became either accepted or tabooed, while other behavior was condemned. No philosophers, for instance, attempted to reconcile the fact that only women can give birth, a matter of female gendered behavior, with their claim that *tian* gave birth to the people and to the world, despite the depiction and correlation of *tian* with maleness as opposed to femaleness.

Although often portrayed now as universalistic and somehow neutral in its perspective, *yinyang* thinking, as it functioned for about two thousand years in Chinese society and values, was, like philosophical thinking, constructed from a male perspective and belonged to a male discourse. With this perspective built into its very concepts, it concerned questions about masculinities, not femininities.[22] There was no comparable system constructed from a female perspective and belonging to a female discourse. Women certainly participated in the *yinyang* discourse, but they did so by experiencing the world through male concepts, for the comprehensiveness of *yinyang* thinking precluded alternative conceptual assumptions. The *yinyang* cosmic dimension of gender thinking provided a theoretical way to include women and justify their actual social location by associating them with *yin*, the completing, dark, and low position, as opposed to *yang*, the initiating (birthing?), bright, and high position. Those activities for which actual women often had responsibility, such as household management, were not addressed in the philosophical texts.

Yinyang thinking offered a way not even to acknowledge those views of women's and men's activities that did not derive from the perspective of privileged men, for there was no place to locate such views theoretically. From the perspective of the Confucian-Mencian social ontology, the daily activities of some people, such as washing clothes or taking care of domestic chores, were not activities (that mattered). *Yinyang* thinking thus reinforced cultural characteristics found in the earlier records of the received tradition, namely, the maleness of the philosophical discourse and so also of the subject, and the higher social value placed on the activities of elite men. Later history illustrates this phenomenon of exclusion through a variety of practices that conceived women and other "others" as recipients of action and rendered them oppressed, often by themselves.[23]

Historians note that gender fluidity in Chinese society was not accompanied historically by any significant broadening of social roles or relaxing of moral norms, and indeed the opposite was the case for elite women.[24] That is, the actual social conditions of women became increasingly restrictive as Confucianism developed, especially from the Song period on. This trend was furthered by various structural features of society, one of which was the flourishing of the examination system, which helped reinforce certain social values associated with binary cultural categories like inner and outer (*neiwai* 內外) and *yinyang*. Like *yinyang* thinking, *neiwai* thinking was also constructed from a male perspective and was a male discourse. For instance, in the matter of political participation (open only to males), successful examination candidates who became government officials were, theoretically speaking, outer (*wai*) and so correlated with *yang* and its male association, while those not in government and who failed the exams were inner (*nei*) and so correlated with *yin* and its female associations. At the same time, since designations of the *yin* and *yang* positions depended on the context, this binary thinking also reinforced the social classification of women and the home as inner and *yin*, and men and political affairs as outer and *yang*.

With some notable exceptions, active political participation by women ended during the Han, a time when *yinyang* correlative thinking took hold and the Confucian canon was established. Even women who were politically involved, such as Wu Zhao (625?–706?), who declared herself Emperor of the new Zhou dynasty in 690 (during the late Tang dynasty) and the Dowager Empress Ci Xi (1835–1908), who ruled behind the throne in the late Qing dynasty, entered a political-philosophical discourse in which the subject remained male gendered. Too much out of place, these women were seen as dangerous to the social-political order, although some dimensions of their (female) behavior were not.[25]

Women were praised within the philosophical tradition for certain virtues, the very ones that made them (in varying ways and to varying degrees) invisible, silent, marginal, subordinate, or associated with things that were undesirable, feared, or considered evil. Such judgments were not self-made but were made from a position of privilege. The oppressive practice of footbinding, for instance, made beautiful feet and restricted persons. Women disciplined themselves by carrying out this practice themselves, and so they literally embodied certain values of (patriarchal) society. Footbinding was a reification of both social restrictions constructed for maintaining order and cultural judgments about that which is ugly and evil. Moreover, as we learn from the earliest texts, good and evil were culturally conceived in terms of beautiful and ugly as well as orderly and disorderly. A contemporary transformation is seen in the practice of "voluntary" leg bone stretching, designed to make a person taller and so more socially acceptable but often leaving young men and women partially crippled.[26] Just as Confucian-Mencian thinking in the past claimed, incorporated, and transformed pre-Confucian values and practices, such as gender fluidity, so the post-Confucian world similarly continues these processes.

Although scholars in the fields of Chinese literature, history, religion, and anthropology have provided many insightful analyses relating to gender, the story has just begun to be told in Chinese philosophy. Ellen Marie Chen took an early lead decades ago by discussing how the great mother and motherly love are at the core of early Daoism and its concept of *dao*, but her work has not been followed by a body of studies in philosophy comparable to the developments in other disciplines.[27] If we look across cultures to Western philosophy, however, a simple listing of the philosophical studies would fill volumes, even shelves. To cite but two of thousands of examples, Page duBois has described a process of appropriation and transformation that constructed the ideal philosopher in Platonic thinking, and Laura Inglis and Peter Steinfeld have analyzed how women both disappeared and yet remained critical in the development of Western philosophy.[28]

The questions motivating this study have expanded and changed over time, but they began with an interest in understanding why and how women in Chinese and other cultures have historically supported the elite's value systems despite the fact that these value systems help construct social conditions that are restrictive and oppressive to women in many ways. This is not to say that men are not also restricted in their behavior, because they certainly are. I could only begin to answer my initial questions after first understanding that, and how, Chinese philosophy historically was a discourse about masculine behavior, and secondly understanding that, and how, it constantly incorporated female gendered behavior as it developed. I have concluded that the feminine (especially, maternal) dimension of Confucian-Mencian ideas was one of the factors that enabled women to support, teach, and promote these values. It was by no means the only factor, however. Furthermore, the incorporation of feminine traits into the Confucian-Mencian ideal of masculinity, especially for elite and powerful men, has not led to the participation of women in those spheres of activity most highly valued in society because those social and political institutions remain male gendered. At best, women have been able to appropriate some forms of masculine behavior by engaging in activities similar to those of men. But they have done so in their separately gendered social realms.

Another factor in the support of patriarchal values by women is the lack of genuine alternatives to dominant social values and practices. People who are disadvantaged by social values and institutions believe in and accept them as the way things are, just as much as the privileged do. Moreover, the ways in which people personally adjust to, and learn, their culture's values contribute to how their character or "person" is shaped, and that character in turn interacts with various features of their social life which then confirm the apparent validity of these values. It is difficult to dismantle the coding that prevents the perspective of particular values from being clearly recognized, particularly when that perspective belongs to a privileged elite.

Such ideas appear to have a validity that transcends a particular time, often because they are claimed to be grounded in biological traits or cosmic processes that are assumed to be universal. Alternative interpretations and genuinely competing ideas are often impossible to imagine, and generally they are not readily available to illustrate how seemingly neutral ideas or values actually entail specific gender and class perspectives, as well as theoretical and historical assumptions. If one is to see the world differently, a wholly different set of assumptions has to come into play, including recognition that philosophical discourse, and the social, cultural, and political realm to which the discourse applies, is gendered.

The interpretations I offer have been carefully considered and are open to textual corroboration. My account is based primarily on the text of *Mencius* itself and secondarily on a few related, relevant texts. The ideas I present are found in the texts, sometimes hidden in plain view and other times not even hidden. However, one has to look in order to see, and what I present here has not usually been looked for, as translations of *Mencius* into English indicate. Since previous translations have been done from a perspective that has much in common with that of Mencius himself, they obscure the very points that I want to bring into awareness. Although it can be made visible, the textual evidence that I cite remains invisible if most cultural rules (Chinese and Western) are followed.

In addition, my methodology of focusing on social relationships and practices, and not on abstract ideas, is a widespread form of Chinese thinking itself. The classic of *Changes* (*Yijing* 易經), for instance, is organized around sixty-four hexagrams, which represent situations that are continually changing. The poems of the *Odes* focus on situations, some political and many personal, as they express the thoughts and feelings of the writers, many of whom claimed to be women (whether true or not). The classic of *Documents* (*Shujing* 書經), the *Record of Rites* (*Liji* 禮記), and many other texts also illustrate this concern with activities and practices. From a philosophical viewpoint, the use of a context or set of practices to establish a frame of reference, which then provides a set of assumptions, associations, and guidelines for thinking, is a feature of Chinese culture. It is an approach that Chinese thinkers and writers themselves used.

One result of studies that have brought out the viewpoint of an "other" has been to remind us that how we conceive and discuss the past is based on a particular, not universal, perspective, no matter what our claims may be. For instance, in the field of environmental history, Mark Elvin has shown how the story of Kua Fu's insatiable thirst, found in the *Liezi* 列子 and *Huainanzi* 淮南子, can be interpreted as a story about environmental destruction, rather than about someone who misjudges his own abilities and so attempts to do too much (the traditional view). Francesca Bray's anthropological study demonstrates how places, spaces, work, and the body are not somehow neutral but are encoded with (patriarchal) values and ideas. And Maram Epstein's literary study reveals how gender is used to convey political positions of orthodoxy and protest, rather than simply functioning as an entertaining feature of some stories.[29]

Despite many advances in knowledge and technology, it still remains that who tells the story is also who controls the memory. As the categories that structure accounts and the tellers of the stories change, however, our understandings of the past and present are transformed. Our perspectives and questions depend on many unspoken assumptions, just as the concepts and narratives of what we are studying did. Recent studies involving gender, for instance, have addressed dimensions of life that historically were hidden from recognition or treated as unimportant. This scholarship enables us to see what we, as contemporary scholars, and they, the past audience of Chinese texts, have been taught not to see. Taking a perspective outside the master narrative of Chinese philosophy, enables me to present a *Mencius* that is not entirely familiar and to uncover some of the implicit ways elite Chinese culture taught people to understand the world.

Gender is one of the most fundamental cultural ordering patterns that seem so natural people are generally not aware that they know them. Gender is still often dismissed as irrelevant. Appropriating from and transforming female gendered behavior, as well as tacitly using the feminine in argumentation, were aspects of the conflicts over changing norms of masculinity, and these aspects and conflicts were both known and unknown. In contrast, comparable conflicts over norms of femininity did not exist in philosophical writings. Although we can only speculate, appropriating from the feminine is perhaps tied to preliterate (prehistorical) changes in the power or status of some women in relation to some men. The traces of such hypothesized changes barely survive but are suggested by the ongoing worldwide traditions of female deities, such as the Chinese Queen Mother of the West, the female deities of Hinduism and Buddhism, and the Christian view of the mother of Jesus as the Mother of God.

On an explicit level, I read *Mencius* as instructing men on how to behave in new ways. If they already were behaving in these ideal ways, this kind of instruction would not have been needed and most likely would not have appeared. As Mark Edward Lewis has suggested, the teachings of this and similar texts were creating an ideal world that did not exist.[30] Plato's ideals have a similar significance. Although much of Mencian thought is stated in the form of descriptions of behavior, these statements are actually prescriptions of what men ought to do. We should also be cognizant that, at the same time that *Mencius* advocates new behavior that is criticized by some as not sufficiently strong and masculine, and perhaps even seen as somewhat weak and feminine, this text provides a strong defense of patriarchy.

A final issue to note briefly is the power of words and a culture's fundamental assumptions about them. When we try to assign a familiar word to situations or practices that may not be recognized as even existing from a privileged cultural perspective, both in Chinese and English, we are immediately confronted with resistances of belief and language. It is often difficult to apply ordinary words in everyday use to activities viewed as unusual, because words are social entities and they contain within themselves specific perspectives. Whether we approve or not, words have meanings beyond our specific references and intended uses, and they belong to those other ontologies too.

For example, the words father and mother may seem to be an appropriate pair, but when viewed in terms of many social practices, they are not, for the practices called fathering and mothering in English do not function in complementary situations. A father can mother, but a mother can never father. Except for breast-feeding and giving birth, a man can feed, bathe, and otherwise take care of a child, but a woman cannot inseminate. In Chinese we find something comparable. The Chinese term *yang* 養 has various meanings, including to nourish in a broad sense or specifically to breast-feed. Similarly, *sheng* 生 entails a range of meanings, including to give birth, produce, or provide sperm. While *Mencius* exhorts a man to *yang* his parents, wife, and children, *Xunzi* points out in one passage that a father cannot *yang* (breast-feed, nourish) but can *sheng* (give birth to, beget) a child, and a mother can feed but cannot instruct.[31] Here we see how critical interpretation and translation are. Another brief example occurring in English and Chinese, and relevant to this study, is that we can talk about the ruling that the ruler does but not about the wife-ing that the wife does, unless we change the vocabulary to words like helping, responding, and serving. Thus we see how a perspective and a social context is built into a word itself.

These examples touch on the difficulties faced in trying to take the perspective of other voices within a particular social ontology, whether that attempt involves making an outsider or non-subject (such as wife) into a subject, attempting to recover voices that have been silenced, or attempting to speak from a different social discourse.[32] Cultures and their texts work against the effort to recover some types of memory but are never able to silence other positions completely, because the other is built into the discourse and the contexts. It is always there, recognized or not. My aim is to help bring these others into our awareness.

Chapter 2

Text As Cultural Landscape

Gender References

Although certain kinds of masculine behavior are the critical concern of Mencius and the activities of men are his explicit focus, women and feminine behavior appear throughout the text, and female behavior is essential to the development of his philosophical ideas about masculinity. To support these claims, I suggest that we first conceive the text in a specific and nontraditional way. That is, view it as a landscape, a cultural landscape, rather than only as a treatise advocating certain views. We can then examine features not usually discussed or even noticed. In particular, we can make a gender map of it, marking the specific features indicating gender. Making such a map requires recognizing the ways in which textual references are made to men, women, and gendered behavior of all kinds. It also involves recognizing our own assumptions as readers. These efforts entail matters of cultural and historical coding, which focuses attention on certain things and, in so doing, renders other things temporarily invisible.

Social conventions and meanings as understood by Warring States audiences at the time of Mencius are difficult, and at times impossible, to determine now, but numerous references to gender still can be retrieved from the text. This effort involves attending to such matters as the use of words and particular terms; the extensions of ideas and actions from one context to another; inversion processes that upset hierarchies; associations both subliminal and explicit; omissions; narratives of the past; theoretical argumentation used to support particular ideas; the issue of whose interests and perspectives are represented; and contradictions and impossible demands. Illustrating this last point is the conflict between the expectations of a particular social identity and practicing certain virtues.

For instance, a person cannot exhibit both the morality of a great man and that of a wife as sketched in 3B2, for this passage promotes the view that a great man is a benevolent ruler of the people, he initiates action, and he practices the moral and political way of the sages. The behavior of a great man takes place within, and in reference to, the political context of the empire. In contrast, a moral wife must be obedient and respectful to her husband. Although her behavior has political implications, it occurs within the context of her family. Their differing existential contexts are part of the meaning of who they are and what they do. Not only can they not adopt each other's actual behavior, a great man and a moral wife live in different cultural and social space-times.

The explicit subject matter of *Mencius* is the empire, the welfare of the people, the good governing of the state, and the moral cultivation of the ruler and the gentleman (*junzi*, less commonly *shi* 士). Ideally, the ruler will become a gentleman. These topics pertain to the interests, occupations, and specific social and moral duties of elite men. The text is silent concerning ideas from the perspectives of the interests and activities of others, such as elite women, the people (*min* 民), or cultural outsiders. The audience receiving the teachings consists of rulers, students and followers, advisors, governors, officials, men from elite families, and other philosophers (all men). They are all somehow involved in governmental affairs, whether actually or potentially. Their occupation, or social role, is to govern.[1] Although many of the text's teachings are about the people or women in some way, neither belongs to the audience or participates in the conversations. The people are prominent in the text as the concern of the advice given to the ruler, but they remain the recipients of the ruler's actions.[2]

Given its perspective, the ideas in *Mencius* assume a division between the ruling elite, or the men (*ren* 人), and the people (*min*). Those "above" and those "below" each have their own activities to carry out, and the moral weight of what they do is judged in reference to the overall social-political order. What one ought to do depends upon where one fits into the social order, according to such considerations as one's work, sex, and family position. Many passages express the view that specific teachings concerning proper action are not applicable to everyone. One such example addresses the difference in proper behavior for Zengzi and Zisi, who were followers of Confucius (and were elites). Both men were facing the same dangerous situation of invaders' coming, but Zengzi was a teacher, considered to be like a father and an older brother, and so he left to escape the outlaws. Zisi was an official, who is subordinate to the ruler, and so he stayed to help his ruler protect his state. Each did what was right for someone in his position

(4B31). In addition to emphasizing the particularity of appropriate behavior, this passage illustrates how gender is carried in the very subject matter and perspective of the text, for the actions offered as examples apply specifically to male gendered behavior.

An example indicating the elite and male subject of the text occurs in a passage that speaks about the three delights of a gentleman (7A20). This passage states that his delights are that his father and mother both remain alive and his older and younger brothers do not cause him concern; in looking up, he is not ashamed (*bukui* 不愧) before *tian* (social conditions and context), and in looking down, he is not ashamed (*bucuo* 不怍) before men; and he is able to teach and nourish (*jiaoyu* 教育) the most talented young men (*yingcai* 英才) of the empire (*tianxia* 天下). Ruling the empire as a benevolent king is not one of his three delights. These four possible pleasures form a single coherent set of situations, with the same one person as the subject of all of them. Their content indicates that they are not the delights of just anyone, but someone with a specific cultural and gender identity, namely the gentleman. Women and the people (commoners) cannot be the audience of this passage since their social obligations prevent them from engaging in this set of activities in its entirety.

Given that cultural associations provide implicit references to male and female gendered behavior, we see that a tacit feminine contribution to Mencius' ideal of masculinity is indicated by the fact that here the gentleman, a potential ruler, values his personal and family relations more than his expected political activities as ruler.[3] The gentleman's delights concern his being a good son, a good brother, a good teacher and nurturer to the best students, and not being ashamed about his behavior. The first two pleasures reflect the results of the kind of childhood learning he would have mastered within the family, the domain of the mother for teaching her young children familial responsibilities, while the third suggests his following the model of his mother in her teaching and nurturing (i. e., feeding). Feelings of shame are applicable to both men and women, but the reasons for their shame are not the same and the differences are important in Mencian thought.

Specific words also indicate gender throughout the text. For instance, when appearing by itself, the term *ren* (man, but often translated in a nongendered way as human being or person) in most cases refers to elite men and excludes elite women and the people. We know this by considering who the subject is, given the context and kind of activity within it. The term *min* (the people) similarly refers most often to adult males specifically, not to women, children, or others among the people, such as elderly parents. Such references are demonstrated in those passages that make women and parents the recipients of others' actions, with phrases like "their wives and children" and "their fathers and mothers."[4] Occupations that are recognized in the text as critical to the Mencian theoretical social order (officials, farmers, artisans, merchants) and other widely recognized kinds of work and activities are understood to be practiced by men, not women, and so are male gendered.[5] In addition, terms used to refer to people in descriptive ways, with or without the suffix *zhe* 者 (one who), most often refer to males, not females, as the contexts confirm.[6] Although exceptions can be found in the text, it is clear that they are exceptions. These types of gender references are obscured, however, in most translations of *Mencius* into English.[7]

That women and certain characteristics of female behavior are present throughout the text can be seen in other ways too. Silences are difficult to interpret fully, for they can have many reasons, but in some contexts exclusion is one form of presence, especially when we know women were present in a particular situation. The most common explicit terms in *Mencius* that refer to females are *nü* 女 and *nüzi* 女子 (woman, daughter, girl, female, wife), *qi* 妻 (wife), *qizi* 妻子 (wife and children, wife), *mu* 母 (mother, female), *pifu* 匹婦 (commoner woman-wife), *shiqie* 侍妾 (female attendant and concubine), *qiefu* 妾婦 (concubine and wife), and *fu* 婦 (wife, lady). A female child or daughter is referred to by a term that qualifies the word for child (*zi* 子), thus indicating that *zi* implicitly means male child unless otherwise specified. For example, in 3B2 and 3B3, a female kind of child, a daughter, is called *nüzi*. We know from the context that *nüzi* means daughter in these two passages, but in other contexts *nüzi* can refer to other kinds of females or female behavior. A son is here called *zhangfu* 丈夫 (young man), not *nanzi* 男子 (male child). Ideally, he will develop himself into a great man (*dazhangfu* 大丈夫), a gentleman and benevolent ruler, while she will be married (*jia* 嫁). As a husband, a man is here called a *fuzi* 夫子, but Mencian teachings do not examine his behavior in that position in any extended philosophical way.

The mention of things culturally associated with females is a further way of referring to them, just as it is with males. Women are associated with the work of weaving, with things like water and valleys, with maternal events such as babies and maternal feelings, and with a subordinate's kind of behavior linked to the social role of wife. Some of the female characteristics appearing in the text conflict with others. Women are linked to evil through such topics as sexual desire, their supposed challenges to the patriarchal family, and disasters. They are linked to compassion and kindness through assumptions about motherhood, and they are linked to that which is subordinate through the role of wife. In a comparable way, other ideas, actions, and things are associated with males and so are male gendered. Making a gender map from the textual landscape thus involves examining the contextual features of the terms and ideas and recognizing the importance of context for determining meaning.

Practices and Relations

My approach is to examine the philosophical ideas in terms of social practices, contexts, and human relationships. I see the Mencian philosophical position as one that entails proposals first to modify certain practices (or modify the contexts that the practices form) and second to modify certain human relationships. The two contexts, or practices, targeted for change are those of farming and of ruling. The practices of the people constitute the context of farming, while the practices of the ruler along with the social-political relations of the ruling elite (commonly known as the five relations) make up the context of ruling. The human relationships targeted for change are those between the ruler and the people and, by the last layer of the text, those that make up the five relations. In other words, the social contexts and human relations that are to be modified involve changes in ideas about the ruler, the people, and those in the five relations, that is, the ruling elite class.

The text rarely utilizes the category human being in the sense of all humans as a group contrasted to other kinds of living things, or in the sense of an individual person without a specific social identity. The first distinction is not an issue of philosophical dispute and the second makes no sense, given philosophical assumptions. Mencius and others assume that gentlemen differ, and ideally all men should differ, from animals and that the more men lack the distinctions of social order, the closer they are to animals.[8] Moreover, the text focuses on humans in specific social ways, that is, in specific kinds of relationships and contexts. In considering the world and masculine behavior from a social-political perspective, Mencian thought pays attention to different types (of human beings or men), types that are differentiated primarily on the basis of socially recognized occupations, behavior, and relations. Given the Mencian ontology, which is a social ontology that designates the elite men (*ren*) and the people (*min*) as two main categories, the text rarely refers to an individual person without a specific social identity, since a particular set of social conditions are critical to who one is and one's social identity provides the context for evaluating behavior.

There are a few examples in which *ren* (man, men), used alone or in a compound, includes the people and the elite, but the distinction between them is also maintained. One such example is Mencius' comment that the difference between men (*ren*) and animals is small (4B19). The commoners (*shumin* 庶民) let it go, but the gentlemen (*junzi*) preserve it. The philosophical point is to contrast the differing behavior of the two fundamental categories of men, the multitudes of the people and the gentlemen.[9] This passage differs from one in which the use of *ren* refers to men only of the elite class, since they constitute the audience of the text (6A15). Mencius claims there that both great men (*daren*) and petty men (*xiaoren* 小人) are equally men (*ren*), but depending on what part of themselves they value, some are great men and some are petty men.[10]

The moral distinction between great men and petty men is also embodied in occupational and class distinctions. In 3A4 (a later passage than 6A15 and discussed below), great men are contrasted to inferior men (*xiaoren*) or the people, and the sage (*shengren* 聖人) to the (men of the) people (*minren* 民人). Thus, the morality of *daren* and *xiaoren* is exhibited both in what men value and in their occupations. Ruling the empire has higher value than farming or carpentry. This expansion in meaning in later textual layers supports the claims of others that the meanings of at least some terms in *Mencius* did change over the period of its compilation. Still, in all these instances, *ren* refers to men, since elite women are not gentlemen, commoners or inferior men, or the people, who are farmers, artisans, and merchants. In most passages, moreover, a social context is indicated or implied, and this context is not separable from a person's behavior and identity.

In order to bring out the specific importance of women's practices and thinking given the lack of explicit philosophical interest in women's activities in *Mencius*, I focus on the social contexts reformulated by Mencius, that is, the practices of farming and ruling, and the social relationships reformulated by Mencius, that between the ruler and the people and those among the five relations. While I maintain that feelings as well as practices are a necessary component of the processes of thinking, a position also strongly claimed in *Mencius*, a comment of Sara Ruddick provides an introductory summary of the connection between practices and thinking:

> From the practicalist view, thinking arises from and is tested against practices. Practices are collective human activities distinguished by the aims that identify them and by the consequent demands made on practitioners

> committed to those aims. The aims or goals that define a practice are so central or "constitutive" that in the absence of the goal you would not have that practiced . . . People more or less consciously create a practice as they simultaneously pursue certain goals and make sense of their pursuit.[11]

The five relations and the practices that constitute them can be distinguished from others by certain criteria. In particular, from a social viewpoint, each relation has social tasks to accomplish as successfully as possible, and these tasks generally involve numerous secondary tasks as well. Certain competencies are required to accomplish the tasks, and these competencies are attained in various ways, depending on the specific practices. Along with having particular goals, each relation involves other expectations. Furthermore, the various relations and their practices function as implicit markers of such traits as gender, class, age, and ethnicity. Given certain practices, people know that the persons involved have certain features. Nothing needs to be said openly at any particular historical time, although such knowledge may be lost to later readers.

The two sets of practices, farming and ruling, have their own relevant standards for making judgments, since the standards by which success is judged vary according to the practices and the specific goals, competencies, and expectations. For instance, the level of accomplishment acceptable in harvesting may be quite different from that of tax collection. Practices are also not static, despite the continuing use of the same terms. While providing a type of continuity, terms of reference imply a uniformity and permanence that does not and did not exist in actual experience. As social conditions changed, different activities became incorporated into older practices and relationships.

A focus on relations and their practices helps prevent ideas from becoming disembodied and removed from their social moorings. It helps to keep in view gender, occupation, and other social dimensions of ideas, particularly those whose social specificity is masked. Since ideas are grounded in particular practices and feelings, all ideas are connected with the practices and feelings of one or more specific relation, although the connections may be long forgotten by later readers. While criteria vary, all practices also include some people and exclude others, and so their ideas apply to some people and not to others. This is rarely said explicitly, much less mentioned every time a specific idea is addressed. Still, their social specificity is an important, although tacit, aspect of the philosophical ideas themselves.

Mencian thought is very much based on the dynamics of interpersonal relations, with maternal practices being especially important. It appropriates ideas from maternal practices (which are not of philosophical concern) and applies them to other contexts that are of concern. The context of farming plays a critical role in the transformation and transfer of maternal ideas. Since some aspects of farming are addressed openly in Mencian philosophy, similarities between maternal and farming practices enable Mencius and his followers (in awareness or not) to draw on maternal practices and thinking while speaking explicitly about farming. The two kinds of practices are transcoded. When the text explicitly discusses farming, it also implicitly speaks about maternal matters. In this way the topic of farming contributes to the process by which Mencian philosophical thought is invisibly structured by concerns, conditions, and values of maternal practices and thinking.

Historically, mothers and sons had important personal relations in actual life, and the relationship between maternal practices and explicit philosophical teachings was significant. The ideas associated with the heart (heart-mind) in *Mencius* are the textual focal point of the maternal dimension, and in my view these ideas are a primary reason of the text's continuing appeal from the Song period on. Without being acknowledged as maternal related, ideas linked to the heart were incorporated into other important concepts, such as "human disposition, tendencies, nature" (*xing* 性), pattern or principle (*li* 理) and "constantly producing" (*shengsheng-yousheng* 生生又生), a central idea in the classic of *Changes*. It is also possible that in rejecting the Mencian concept of the heart-mind, Xunzi and certain other thinkers were implicitly discrediting ideas that most people knew to be true from their own experiences.

As a further observation concerning the analysis of this text, it is important to remember that the official view throughout history maintained that farming is the basis of the state. While the importance of farming is incontrovertible, the conviction itself (as distinct from actual human needs) that farming is the fundamental occupation was likely strengthened by its implicit associations with maternal practices, which are fundamental to humans and animals. The theoretically unrecognized maternal dynamics within Confucian thought conceivably contributed to women's support of classical values because they were familiar to mothers. Mothers knew the values made sense from their own experiences.

Maternal Practices and Thinking

The lack of direct statements in the text makes it necessary to turn to other sources both in and beyond the text to reconstruct maternal thinking and practices in Mencian thought. Close reading of the text suggests that there are indeed genuine philosophical reasons, beyond the anecdotes, for the later value accorded Mencius' mother and other mothers in the cultural tradition. In addition, studies by historians and anthropologists provide help for interpreting contexts and content of the text, and feminist philosophers offer methodological guides. Other fields are relevant too, especially psychology and literary and cultural criticism. Cultural associations, the argumentation in the text, the language and terms used, references in other texts, and cross-cultural studies all contribute clues and suggestions. While the picture I offer has more to be added, it provides a way to consider the relationship of women (as mothers and wives) to the philosophical tradition and a way to think about competing forms of masculinities.

Characteristics of maternal thinking and practices exhibit considerable historical and cultural differences in time and place. Regardless of the differences, however, maternal thinking was of no more interest to traditional philosophers in China than in Europe. Until very recently, the tradition of Eurocentric philosophy simply did not recognize it as an area for examination. Male philosophers developed concepts and theories based on their own experiences, which did not include the maternal practices of giving birth and breast-feeding. Not seen as having a defining logic, maternal thinking clearly fell short of Western philosophical standards of rationality and abstraction. For instance, even when Kant distinguished practical reason from pure reason, the former did not measure up to the latter in moral worth. Only in the latter half of the twentieth century did writers begin to treat the topic of maternal experiences as worthy of philosophical examination.

Focusing on how maternal practices differ from other social practices in the West, Adrienne Rich and Sara Ruddick were among the first to claim that a certain kind of thinking is involved that is related specifically to the aims and practices of motherhood, that "maternal thinking is one kind of disciplined reflection among many, each with identifying questions, methods, and aims."[12] The logic of maternal thinking has certain characteristics that distinguish it from other kinds of thinking, such as scientific, legal, and political thinking. Since it has its own standards for determining and evaluating its practices, standards that derive from its own specific goals, maternal thinking may appear deficient when judged by scientific or rationalistic philosophical standards. On the other hand, it is now widely recognized that the standards of any particular kind of thinking, including scientific thinking, are not applicable to all kinds of practices, for practices vary in respect to aims. Differences in practices do not prevent aspects of one kind of thinking from being applied to another kind of thinking, however. Appropriations of this sort are widely seen in Chinese and Eurocentric philosophy and indeed may be one of the sources of philosophical creativity.

I am thus proposing that the dynamic of borrowing and transformation was an important aspect of philosophical creativity in ancient China, although not explicitly recognized. This dynamic worked through processes based on association and metonymy. Both Confucian and Daoist (male) thinkers adapted characteristics of maternal practices and thinking to their own political, social, and religious interests. They appropriated the logic, along with certain views and assumptions, of maternal thinking but did not identify them as such. In effect, the original practitioners (mothers) themselves were silenced while (a transformed version of) their thinking was not. Various early texts contain enough clues to recontextualize patterns of thinking transferred from the maternal to the ruling context. For instance, we see that the language of maternal activities became used in the context of governing. Moreover, since the farming context was a critical component of the Mencian views of governing, it served as a continuing important link, as noted above. From a theoretical viewpoint, women's behavior is incorporated into the behavior of men.

Females differ greatly in their sociocultural conditions and in their motivations, but most share certain biological features.[13] Only females have the potential capability to give birth and to breast-feed a baby. Whether fulfilled or not, this natural potential does not limit in theory what else a female can do, but it does indicate male limitations.[14] Events such as birth and breast-feeding take place in widely varying social circumstances, for motherhood is cultural as well as biological. Both biological and cultural factors are critical, interdependent, and often cannot be truly separated. It may not even be possible to distinguish between the two, since how events are experienced and interpreted is mediated through one's culture, including the categories themselves of biological and cultural.

Some cultures assume that maternal love and commitment are inborn in the mother, but contemporary and historical data raise serious doubts about such beliefs. Ruddick, along with others, claims that:

> . . . maternal commitment is far more voluntary than people like to believe. Women as well as men may refuse to be aware of or to respond to the demands of children; some women abuse or abandon creatures who are, in all cultures, dependent and vulnerable.[15]

In other words, many factors, both cultural and personal, contribute to how the young are treated.

The issue of ancient Chinese assumptions about maternal love is critical to the philosophical claims I make in this study. I interpret *Mencius* to be making the then radical claim that although the culture assumes this kind of love and commitment is inborn only in women as future mothers, that assumption is only partly true, for it is also inborn in men. This latter claim—that men also innately have these so-called maternal characteristics, especially love and compassion—is what makes Mencian views concerning the heart philosophically and historically important. My hypothesis is strengthened by the cultural assumption already prevalent that, speaking metaphorically, men have the ability to give birth—not to babies themselves, but as rulers to the conditions that make social and political life possible.

Other questions about maternal love and commitment can be asked in addition to whether or not love and commitment are inborn. Another important question is whose love and commitment is it actually. Since societies vary in terms of their family systems and in terms of who has authority for making certain family decisions, it likely that the location of maternal commitment varies too. It may not lie in the biological mother of the baby, as is widely believed by many at present. It may, for instance, lie in the grandmother or grandfather or other members of an older generation.

Contemporary individualistic views often lead people simply to assume that commitment and motivation are located in an individual person, in the one who supposedly acts. But there are many reasons for thinking that this was neither the case in ancient China nor is it now. Not only did the Chinese historically not have the concept of an individual person as a self-contained entity who could act autonomously, other cultures past and present have taken, and still take, a more interactive view of what a person is. Mencian emphases on personal motivation and commitment presented challenges to widespread cultural assumptions by allowing some persons, namely, gentlemen, to go beyond common practices. His ideas were in some ways counter-cultural. Similarly, his claim that maternal commitment, symbolically condensed into his conception of the heart and its related theories, is natural in men too, not just in women, was a radical position. By drawing on analogies such as Ox Mountain, he conveys this message through multiple links of associations (6A8).

According to Ruddick's analysis, maternal practices have several goals from the mother's viewpoint, or demands from the baby's viewpoint, which may be grouped and categorized in various ways. Ruddick discusses three goals, or demands, that make up maternal work: preservation, growth or nurturance, and social acceptability or training. In the following discussion, I apply her analysis to *Mencius*, with some change in emphasis and an expansion of the goals to four by explicitly adding birth.

From the mother's or family's viewpoint, the first goal is the successful birth of the baby, along with the mother's survival and the baby's good health. A period of preparation of some sort ideally leads to the baby's birth. The pre-*Mencius* Confucian *Analects* and post-*Mencius* texts such as the *Liji* (*Record of Rites*) comment on the expectant mother's behavior and her prenatal teaching. Second is the goal of the baby's preservation. A baby is vulnerable, endangered by many things, and requires protection to survive. It is significant that the way of the *ru* (Confucian) was openly compared to caring for a baby (3A5).[16] Third is the goal of nurturing, taking care of the baby, and helping it to grow. The baby not only must survive but must be taken care of in order to grow, develop, and mature. Ideally the mother or those persons responsible want to nurture and rear the child as safely and effectively as possible, although this may not always be the case and may not happen. A child's growth may conflict with his or her survival. Terms like *bao* 保, protect and nourish, figure prominently in Mencian vocabulary, thus reflecting this goal.

Fourth, the child needs to become acceptable to society, so that the child and the parents will not be dangerous to others or be rejected and killed by others. In other words, a child's learning to become socially acceptable is a matter of survival for the parents and family, for the child, and for society. Mothers or those with maternal responsibility are thus involved in the early process of education and training, so that the young child learns proper social behavior. Mothers and caretakers use many strategies, and many types of education occur, from the child's learning the spoken language and how to behave in a bodily and communicative sense with others, to learning values and numerous cultural and conceptual distinctions. The need for the child to gain social acceptability may be full of conflicts for the mother, for she may not agree with all the social values and practices that she teaches her child, but the child must learn them nonetheless to live successfully in, and not destroy, society.

Different aspects of maternal work may not be practiced by, or be the responsibility of, the birth mother in all cases and cultures, but the work itself is necessary and must be done by someone. We know that in elite Chinese society, for instance, the birth mother did not necessarily do any or all of the maternal work. The distinction between birth mother and social mother has long been made, and servants did much of the essential work among the elite of taking care of the baby, including breast-feeding.

To achieve the goals of maternal work, mothers or those responsible need to do more than just care about the child or act from "natural" impulses. A mother must think about what to do and to follow up her thinking with appropriate actions. As Ruddick points out, "The discipline of maternal thought like other disciplines, establishes criteria for determining failure and success, sets priorities, and identifies virtues that the discipline requires."[17] In other words, maternal work establishes a kind of thinking that is relevant to its own aims, conditions, and practices.

As further discussion will explain, Mencian thought borrowed the type of thinking associated both with maternal practices and with the practices of the role of wife in ancient China, and applied such thinking to the non-maternal and non-wifely practices of governing, despite the latter's different aims. Drawing selectively on the cultural tradition, Mencian thought developed concepts about, and expanded to a broader arena, the goals, priorities, virtues, strategies, and practices of the maternal situation. While it would be impossible to say how aware the authors and compilers were of what they were doing, passages like that cited above in this and other texts indicate that at least some people saw a maternal connection.

Interpreting *Mencius* from this perspective requires the contemporary reader to be willing to go beyond a narrow reading that focuses primarily on what the text seems to say explicitly in a particular passage. Other passages and other aspects of the cultural and social context must be kept in mind, as well as the processes by which human beings think and form ideas. The role of associations in forming ideas is an example of these processes and is especially important. To say this another way, and here I borrow from Michael Nylan, "beliefs about certain topics . . . do not exist as isolated clusters . . . ," but form "endless chains of connected thoughts from which we construct meaning in our lives, with one topic sliding, almost unnoticed, into another."[18] Taking into account this notion of "endless chains," I suggest that a variety of characteristics of the text, including the examples and analogies that are used, the cultural ideas associated with them, and the use of quotations, all contribute to my thesis that the Mencian position regarding masculinity derives in a fundamental way from maternal experience. The prominent markers of this position are the ideas about the heart, the four beginnings, the virtues, the benevolent ruler, and benevolent government.

Farming Practices and Thinking

In *Mencius* farming is regarded as the fundamental occupation of the people, and the people's occupation is the base of the state. The practices of farming are conceived broadly and include various activities in addition to agricultural work in the fields. Since both the agricultural and other practices have certain characteristics similar to those of maternal practices, the similarities enabled a constant, although not usually acknowledged, association to be made. A politically useful slippage of ideas between the maternal and farming contexts exists, so that talk about farming, whatever aspect, implicitly elicits ideas that are associated with maternal practices and thinking, which are not talked about.

Farming in the sense of agriculture has goals or demands (depending on the viewpoint) that are comparable to the first three of maternal practices, while a fourth goal diverges. The farmer's first goal is that the seeds sprout. The farmer thus readies the soil in various ways. Once the seeds have germinated, the farmer must respond to the young sprouts' need to be preserved and protected from various dangers, such as hungry animals or unseasonable weather. Third, the farmer must nurture the plants, by such actions as weeding, fertilizing, and watering. Finally the plants must ripen and be harvested for eating. This fourth goal does not entail teaching, as in the maternal context, but it does involve making the crops acceptable for eating. Although the concerns are different, the farmer, like the mother, may have ambivalence regarding this goal, for the finer his harvested crops are, the more taxes he will have to pay. Planting mulberry trees so that the leaf-eating silkworms can be raised is also a farming activity, and it leads to women's work of spinning and weaving. The trees and silkworms involve goals and require a type of active involvement similar to growing crops.

In addition to growing crops, raising silkworms, and weaving, other farming activities include hunting, fishing, trapping, woodcutting, raising domestic animals for food, and instruction on filial, fraternal, and respectful behavior to one's superiors. Military service is also required. Although the goals and kinds of thinking in many of these activities are similar to those of agricultural work and sericulture, they entail a different kind of human involvement. In these latter cases, humans contribute better to the goals of birth, preservation, and nurturing by not interfering with non-domesticated creatures at critical times in their lives. Agriculture and sericulture require appropriate involvement, but hunting and woodcutting require restraint. Various textual passages suggest that the range of farming activities did not translate into economic well-being for the people. Rather, the people's lives were very difficult, characterized by starvation and desperate attempts to survive.

The characteristics of these practices in both the maternal and farming contexts make certain types of thinking necessary for success. The implicit associations between maternal and agricultural thinking are based on the fact that both are concerned with living things. Both kinds of practices entail the need to recognize and work in harmony with patterns of the natural world beyond human control. Mencian thought accepts that living things have their own rhythms that are necessary for their existence. As Mencius commented in one conversation (6A9), even a plant that is easy to grow will not be able to survive if it has warm conditions for one day but cold for ten. If their fundamental patterns are ignored or violated by human beings, crops will fail and silkworms, fish, turtles, and trees will die. Thus, in dealing with living things, whether plants or animals, success depends on the adaptation by those who are stronger and more powerful to the life requirements of the weaker. Use of overpowering force will lead to eventual failure and disaster, as the man from Song demonstrated when he "helped" his crops to grow by pulling them up a little (2A2).

Concerned with living and growing things, those involved in maternal and farming practices must think in terms of certain issues in order to succeed. Such issues include timing and timeliness; appropriateness of one's actions; a consideration of whether conditions are controllable or uncontrollable, predictable or unpredictable; constancy in one's nurturing efforts; and nurturing and guiding rather than forcing. Success requires a recognition that living things have certain tendencies inherent in them, which can be encouraged and guided in development or crushed and cut off. Thus, adherence to fixed or purely abstract standards cannot be the highest value in this kind of thinking if one is to be successful. Adaptation to changing and unpredictable conditions is necessary, whether these conditions entail the soil and the weather or the plants and the tiller himself.

There are of course important differences between the two contexts. The crops and animals emerge from the soil and animals; they belong to some other category of thing, something nonhuman. In contrast, a mother gives birth to and nurtures one of her own kind. Secondly, her own and her family's expectations, attitudes, and feelings toward the child differ from the way a farmer thinks about his crops, animals, or the wood he cuts. Although these relationships are not simple matters, there is no indication in the text that a farmer has compassion, for instance, for his crops in the way mothers are assumed to have for their young children.

While the text speaks of farming in a broad sense with a variety of activities, the more restricted agricultural terms *nong* 農 (to farm), *geng* 耕 (to till, plow), and *nou* 耨 (to weed) are the usual terms of reference, deriving from the primary occupational practice. Used most often, the term *nong* itself reinforces the gender and class dimensions of farming, for along with *shi* (gentleman), *gong* 工 (artisan), and *shang* 商 (merchant), *nong* (farmer) is one of the four classes of men noted above. As male gendered, they function in the outer (*wai*) sphere of society, not the inner (*nei*) sphere of family. The text occasionally mentions other categories of work, but the contexts make it clear that the workers belong to one of the four types. For example, in 1A7, the text mentions gentlemen in the empire, tillers, merchants, travelers, and political dissenters in the empire. The first and last of these types are from the elite; the others from among the people. Travelers are involved in trade; they are not vacationers. The four types point to occupations, which help construct the social system in terms of class.

The very specificity of these occupational terms contributes to establishing and maintaining the Mencian type of patriarchal system. Its social divisions are kept in the forefront by the construction of sharp differences theoretically separating the occupational groups from each other. At the same time, there are strong indications in the text that actual social life was far more complex than the theoretical view. Clear class distinctions, even if hypothetical, are reinforced by clear distinctions (perhaps also hypothetical) among the five relations. We should note that just as the concept of the five relations simplifies the complexities of interpersonal experiences, the term *nong* silences a variety of farming activities by foregrounding agriculture.

In sum, Mencian thinking reinvents two kinds of existing practices, and these Mencian reinventions are implicitly based on thinking deriving from, or similar to, that of maternal practices. The two reinventions are the practices of the people, in shorthand referred to as farming, and the practices of the ruling elite, which focus on their social-political relations, that is, the five relations. Although the text does not make any explicit linkage, its discussion about the people's work and about the five relations also provides an implicit discussion about maternal practices, since the former elicits tacit associations with the latter. That is, through the continuing explicit concern in the text with the farming context and with the five relations (with some emphasized more than others), maternal thinking was able to have a continuing invisible presence and influence in the philosophical tradition. These two related clusters of reinventions are the core of the new Mencian concept of benevolent government.

The Mencian position is that the king's implementation of a new political order, one that is more encompassing and more considerate of the people, is an important step toward achieving a benevolent government. A range of actions for the king to implement are proposed in the text, including those that are economic, environmental, ritual, social, and educational. The fact that these proposed actions in various ways concern women as mothers or wives, but without direct mention of them, reinforces the association between the maternal and farming contexts, an association fundamentally based on their mutual concern with living, growing things.

Chapter 3

Against Shen Nong's Agrarian Masculinity

Mencius presents his ideas about the gentleman in many ways. He not only provides specific examples of the behavior he most admires, he also argues against those kinds of behavior that he rejects. To help people better understand his ideas, he often refers to differing masculinities by the names of men who best embodied each kind. While Mencius praised the behavior of Kings Wen and Wu, for instance, he severely criticized that of the followers of Shen Nong and of King Hui of Liang. His arguments against the agrarian masculinity of Shen Nong's followers are presented in this chapter and against the self-centered masculinity of King Hui in the next chapter.

I offer here a close reading of passage 3A4 in order to illustrate in a general way how Mencius uses gender in his argumentation and to examine specifically how and why Mencius argues against Shen Nong's agrarian form of masculinity.[1] Important for its ideas about political and social order, passage 3A4 belongs, according to the Brooks' textual analysis, to the last southern layer of the text, compiled 254–249 BCE, approximately 60–70 years after the original interviews of Mencius, 320–310 BCE. Unlike passages from the earliest layers, this one contains abundant references to female as well as male behavior and so possibly attests to a continuing, although unacknowledged, interest in the gender aspects of philosophical issues.

As the following analysis shows, what I call the agrarian position is one type of masculinity rejected by Mencius because it blurs social and class distinctions based on work and occupation and it focuses on small everyday matters, rather than large matters of the empire. Despite its association with King Wen, whose benevolence is associated with feminine, especially maternal, virtues, Mencius considers agrarian masculinity tainted by its association with other forms of feminine behavior, particularly those that are like a wife's behavior of feeding superiors. Although both the Mencian ideal masculinity and this rejected form have aspects appropriated from female behavior, the traits that they appropriate differ. Superficial similarities between the two forms of masculinity make agrarian behavior especially dangerous to patriarchal order, and so Mencius argues against it in an extensive way.

The passage opens with a reference to a man named Xu Xing, who was a follower of the mythological sage ruler Shen Nong 神農, the Divine Farmer. Xu Xing had traveled from the southern state of Chu north to the state of Teng, where Duke Wen (i. e., King Wen of the Zhou) was reputed to be implementing benevolent government (*renzheng* 仁政). In his request to the Duke to be allowed to live in Teng, Xu Xing marks himself as an outsider, for he tacitly evokes the opening passage of the *Analects* by referring to himself as "a man from afar." Xu's followers are described as wearing clothing of unwoven hemp and as earning a living by making hemp sandals and weaving mats.

So far in this passage about male behavior, references to female behavior are pervasive. An ancient culture hero, the Divine Farmer was known for inventing agriculture and herbal medicine, introducing the concepts of markets and trade, and helping to develop the sixty-four hexagrams of the classic of *Changes*.[2] As such, he implicitly evokes ideas associated with plants and the cultivation of crops, such as fertility, birth, growth, cultivation, and nourishing. These ideas have ancient associations with women in Chinese culture and across the world. The Divine Farmer further suggests the belief among many Chinese elite that farming is necessary to the existence of civilization, for the elite consider people without sedentary agriculture as barbarian. *Shen*, translated as Divine in this name, also has the meanings of spirit and mystery, ideas that are associated with the ultimate source of living things and with *dao* (way). These references both to farming and the divine evoke maternal characteristics of fertility, birth, growth, nourishing, and the mysterious source of life. The Divine Farmer and those who advocate his teachings thus carry buried references to women and female gender, particularly maternal behavior.

The mention of the Chu origin, the clothes, and the occupation of Xu Xing and his followers also associate them and the Divine Farmer with women, although scholars have traditionally interpreted these traits as mainly symbolic of rustics and of a simple life, the opposite of the ideal Confucian world of culture and good government. Women in the role of wife (or wife to be) were the ones who wove cloth and made clothing, but here it is Xu Xing's (male) followers who are described as binding up hemp sandals and weaving mats in order to eat, and who wore coarse, unwoven clothes. They are doing women's type of work. Women themselves are not participants here, since their own work of weaving is not explicitly part of this setting and the fertility and cultivation practices are applied to farming, rather than to human reproduction. Still, the juxtaposition of life producing activities and women's work, done here by men or expressly not done (as in unwoven hemp clothing), provides a tacit female gender dimension to this account of male behavior.

Activities normally carried out by mothers and wives are here appropriated by men who are drawn to Duke Wen's state because of his benevolent government. As will be discussed further below, benevolence is one of the four Mencian virtues and is claimed to develop from compassion, a feeling based in the heart and closely associated with mothers and their maternal feelings toward their children.[3] By practicing benevolent government, Duke Wen has appropriated maternal compassion from within the family and transformed it into political benevolence in the state. Moreover, the implication of Chu as Xu Xing's origin is that Chu is at the southern fringe of the empire. Its culture and government are other, outside the social-political order of the central states. The set of associations thus expands. Xu Xing and his followers literally come from afar. They are outsiders, just as women are theoretically outside the patriarchal order by being outside the discourse concerning male gendered behavior. Their state is peripheral, their work is like women's work, they follow agrarian teachings, which are transcoded with maternal practices, and they are attracted to a benevolent government, just as children rely on their caring mothers.

Following a similar narrative pattern, the next section of this passage speaks about Chen Xiang and his brother, who come to Teng from Song and are described as carrying plows and shares on their backs. That is, they too are farmers and rustics and now want to become subjects of a sage ruler. Their home state of Song was the home of the descendants of Shang dynasty rulers, the dynasty conquered by the Zhou. The mother of King Wen (of the Zhou) also came from the Shang people.[4] A small state, Song had become militarily weak, certainly no contender for interstate power, but in several Mencian passages (3B5, 3B6) it is linked to benevolent government because of its ruler's efforts and its association with the former sagely rulers. Due to its weakness and defeated situation, Song now implies a subordinate, outside, and weak position, as opposed to the superior and strong masculine position in the patriarchal hierarchy. Maternal behavior and female gender are established as a tacit dimension of this section too, through their associations with farming, benevolent government, and a marginal and weak political status.

Chen Xiang and his brother had been followers of Chen Liang, but they now convert to the teachings of Xu Xing and his agrarian position. Advocating Xu Xing's agrarian viewpoint to Mencius, Chen Xiang says that a ruler who truly follows *dao* also tills the land along with the people and cooks his own meals, thus blurring the division of work in terms of both gender and occupational class. The occupational class division described in Mencian thought requires, however, that the people (males) till the soil while the ruler rules. The ideal of gender distinctions (both among the people and the elite) requires women (as wives) to cook and weave, while the elite men govern and the commoner men either farm, do artisan work, or engage in trade.

Mencius responds by arguing against the blurring of boundaries and for a clear division of labor, an argument that is reflected in his distinction here between the affairs of the great men (*daren*) and the affairs of the inferior men (*xiaoren*). Mencius claims that, laboring with their hearts (or heart-minds, *xin* 心), the great men govern and are fed (*shi* 食) by the inferior men. Laboring with their strength, the inferior men are governed and feed the great men. In opposition, Chen Xiang argues that a ruler puts a hardship on the people by not supporting (feeding) himself by working in the fields and instead relying on the people. The people's relationship to the elite is similar to the wife's relationship to her husband, for both the people and wives are in subordinate positions. Moreover, the people are associated with female behavior in that they, like wives, feed others.

Other Mencian passages speak to this occupational, class, and gender divide too. In 3A3, for instance, there is a focus on the governing responsibilities of the elite in regard to "the affairs of the people" (*minshi* 民事). Here the term used is *minshi*, rather than *xiaorenzhishi* (小人之事, the affairs of the inferior men) as in 3A4 above. Several later statements in 3A3 also reflect the Mencian focus on a division of labor and roles. "When the relations of the men (*renlun*) are clear above, the inferior people (*xiaomin* 小民) are affectionate [to their elders] (*qin* 親) below." *Xiaomin* appears in place of *min* or *xiaoren*, and *ren* instead of *daren*. Using the terms gentlemen elite (*junzi*) and rustics or commoners (*yeren* 野人) to make the class distinction, this passage further says, "Without the gentlemen, there will be none to govern the commoners; without the commoners, there will be none to feed (or support *yang*) the elite." In this way Mencius advocates a clear division of labor with a tacit gender dimension indicated in part by the separation of governing from feeding.

To argue against Xu's and Chen's agrarian "leveling" position (in 3A4), Mencius inquires about Xu Xing's own behavior and learns that Xu himself grows the grain that he eats but he trades for other things that he needs. While he wears unwoven hemp clothes, he does trade grain for his silk cap, which is woven, and for the earthenware and iron implements that he uses. Chen defends Xu's trading for these things on the basis that he cannot both till the land and engage in the work of all the crafts. Mencius points out that Xu does not put hardship on the potter and the blacksmith when he trades his grain for their implements, and when they trade their implements for grain, they do not cause the farmer to suffer. And it is the same way with governing the empire. In effect, a ruler trades his work of governing for the necessities of life, and this exchange does not cause the ruled to be oppressed.

But consider what happens to women and women's work here in the course of the argument. This passage at first deals with three kinds of necessities—clothing, food, and implements for eating and plowing. In his argument, however, Mencius focuses only on the two of food and implements. He limits the exchange of work to only the farmer-tillers, potters, and blacksmiths—all occupations of men, and he pays no attention to the weavers and their exchanges. Since ordinarily weavers are women, work related to weavers is dropped from the argument because Mencius is concerned with masculine, not feminine, behavior. The work of weaving is not a craft or occupation like pottery and ironwork. Absorbed into men's activities, women's work, as distinct from the role of wife, is not a theoretical aspect of the social ontology because this patriarchal system is a system of masculinities.

In addition, the agrarian view of Xu Xing advocates that the ruler should prepare his own meals as well as farm the land. Like weaving, cooking is women's work and it is also dropped from Mencius' argument. In other words, the issue of the division of labor, phrased here as the work of the great men and of the inferior men, concerns only masculine behavior. Mencius is troubled only by the possibility of farming while governing, not by the possibility of farming and cooking while governing. Cooking is simply outside the focus of his concerns, since weaving and cooking are not among the hundred crafts (*baigong* 百工) and are not one of the four (occupational) classes.

A similar situation reflecting women's "invisibility" in a gender system of masculinities occurs in 3B4, in which Mencius defends the rightness of the gentleman's exchanging his work for food (or support). In mentioning the work that the various classes of people do, Mencius refers to males by their work and to females by their sex. A farmer (*nong*) grows grain, a woman or his wife (*nü*) weaves cloth, carpenters and carriage makers make things, and a gentleman (*shi*) practices benevolence and rightness (*renyi* 仁義). The latter work is explained as being filial (*xiao* 孝) when inside (the family), deferential (*ti* 弟) when outside, and preserving the (moral) way of the former kings for future students (*xuezhe* 學者). Mencius argues that the carpenters and carriage makers trade their products for food from the farmers, and it is right and not oppressive for the gentleman to do the same. Otherwise, carpenters and carriage makers would be more respected than gentlemen. Mencius' point is that more highly respected (male) behavior is linked to a division of labor, with its resulting exchange of goods and services. If the gentleman's work is not considered as specialized, the gentleman would be like a barbarian or a woman, whose work ignores social distinctions.

Although women's work of weaving is mentioned here at first, when it comes to comparing a gentleman's "right" to eat even though he does not produce food as a farmer does, the comparison is made only with the craftsmen. Like the gentleman, the craftsmen also trade their work for food. Nothing is said of their trading work for clothing or the woman's trading clothing for food. Thus we see, from the argument itself, how gender is built into the philosophical discourse. This example illustrates how Mencian thought is implicitly concerned with "contesting masculinities," which here are represented by the work behavior of gentlemen, craftsmen, farmers, and the agrarian advocates.[5] A condensed statement of this argument also appears in 7A32, where only two kinds of work are mentioned, the farmer's work of tilling the land and the gentleman's work of serving the ruler and of teaching the sons and younger brothers filial, fraternal, loyal, and trustworthy behavior.

Although the explicit subject here is male activities and the value of the division of their labor, maternal practices are implicitly evoked through the associations with farming and teaching. It is understood, moreover, that within this Mencian system to labor with one's heart implies governing with compassion and benevolence, as opposed to force. Thus, in doing this kind of work, the great man or the gentleman tacitly appropriates some traits of maternal behavior and applies them to the political realm.

Reviewing the web of associations that have come into play so far, we see that the heart (or, working with the heart), the great men, gentlemen, certain kinds of moral behavior, and governing are contrasted to physical strength (working with one's strength), the inferior men or the people, and feeding or supporting others. Arguably the central concept in Mencian thought, the heart has a range of meanings that include feeling, aspiring, and thinking. Female gendered feelings, such as compassion and caring, are especially associated with the heart. The "heart work" of women, work seen as naturally involving compassion and love, consists of raising children and taking care of the elderly, weaving, and cooking. Although this work requires skill, it is not artisan work (*gong*) belonging to the masculinities of the patriarchal system. Women themselves are not included in the contrast between the great men and inferior men, but female gendered behavior is. As wives, women of all classes are implicitly linked to the latter set of associations, that of ideas associated with the inferior men—both through their lack of participation in political rule as a subject and through their work of supporting and feeding others through weaving and cooking. On the other hand, women as mothers are implicitly linked to the former set of associations, related to the great men or gentlemen, since mothers' heart work of compassion and kindness to children is transformed here into a ruler's benevolence toward the (inferior) people.

There are still more ideas in passage 3A4. With the aim of defending the Mencian division of labor separating the rulers (the great men) and the people (the inferior men), the next section concerns how the ancient sages and culture heroes, especially Yao, Shun, and Yu, brought order to a world that was not regulated by humans, that is, a realm beyond human society. They did this by instituting a human imposed order on the apparent wildness of the land, waters, animals, and birds. To control and master the conditions of flooding, thick vegetation, and numerous birds and animals, Yao gave authority to Shun, who in turn instructed Yi to burn the mountains and marshes, so that the wild animals had to flee. Yu dredged and diked the rivers to dry out the land for farming. After the land and waters were "subdued" and animals and birds driven away or killed, the people of the central states were able to plant grain to eat. The point is made that for eight years Yu was so busy establishing order that he passed by his own house three times and never went in to visit; so certainly he had no time for farming either.

The natural environment is considered chaotic, hostile, wet, and outside the social order, which is symbolized here by the concept of the central states (*zhongguo* 中國). Therefore it requires regulation and the establishment of boundaries. The inherent and continuing unruliness of nature (mountains, marshes, animals, birds, and rivers) demands a ruler who can focus all of his efforts on governing. A ruler must give all his attention to the affairs of governing because that which is outside (and so threatening to) the social order is inherently and continuingly unruly and overflowing.

Interpreted as dangerous, these conditions are constant and never cease; thus there must be a division of labor between the rulers and the people. As can be seen here, nature and women have some similar characteristics.

Next we read that Hou Ji taught the people how to farm and so the people (*minren*, the commoner men, as opposed to the *shengren*, the sagely men) were nourished (*yu* 育). Scholars disagree on the translation of Hou Ji—whether it should be Lord Millet, Queen Millet, or one who controls the millet, but maternal associations are present.[6] The third possible translation here on the surface desexes this culture hero, but because it has human characteristics, it must be sexed—even if the sex is masked verbally. Farming and maternal practices are linked through teaching, fertility (the ripening of the grains), and nourishing (*yu*). If Hou Ji is a female, the maternal and farming contexts coalesce openly; if a male, the female associations remain, but maternal nurturing characteristics are appropriated and veiled.

The text further claims that the way of men (commoner men) is such that, once they have enough food and warm clothes, they will be like wild animals if they are not given instruction during their leisure time. (The threat of chaos is constant and must constantly be managed.) Given the philosophical context, the term *ren*, translated here as men, clearly refers to men among the people and is a shortened form of the phrase *minren* (commoner men), which occurs just above. As a brief aside here to remind us of what the philosophical context is, the context is twofold: first, Mencius' defense of a social and occupational division between the ruler and the people and, second, the assumption that the people are men, for Mencius is addressing types of male behavior only.

Shun's concern led him to appoint Xie to teach the people the "relations of the rulers" (*renlun*), for unlike the people, the ruling elite recognized social distinctions, which establish and maintain order if practiced. When *renlun* is translated as human relations or the five relations, as it often is, the class and gender dimensions of this concept are suppressed. The context of this account (Mencius' defense of social and occupational divisions) tells us, however, that the relations taught are those of the great men, the ruling elite, as opposed to the inferior men, those who are governed. *Ren* (men) in *renlun* refers to the rulers or gentlemen, for the people are naturally like animals and so "in need" of instruction to participate properly in the Confucian-Mencian social order. Commoner men do not naturally practice distinctions in work and relationships, as the agrarian position reveals. In addition, since the people whom the instruction concerns are males, it is clear that their relations are the ones essential to establishing and confirming the social order. The five relations or relations of the rulers (*renlun*) are a critical and necessary building block of civilization.

These relations stress the kinds of behavior, commonly called moral virtues, that should prevail in particular social contexts, and the appropriateness of the specific behavior in turn ideally constructs the relation in a genuine sense—in behavior as well as in word. The relations to be taught consisted of affection between father and son, dutifulness or rightness between ruler and minister, separateness between husband and wife, proper position between older (brother) and younger (brother), and trustworthiness between friends.[7] Keeping in mind that throughout the text there is an unacknowledged tension between female gendered behavior derived from maternal contexts and the patriarchal order of the social-political world, this statement of these relations reflects a strong affirmation of the patriarchal order, for (inner) family relations consist of three types, which are used to enhance (outer) political relations. A full statement of the five does not occur in *Mencius* until this passage (3A4) from the last layer of the text. Perhaps indicating a more focused concern, the earlier textual layers only refer to the relations of ruler and minister, father and son, and older and younger brother.[8]

The brevity of this statement about *renlun* makes its meaning ambiguous, but the assumptions and beliefs of Mencian thought and that of other thinkers provide a context that enables us to determine significant aspects of its meaning. Since these five relations are part of an order that is fundamentally hierarchical, the obligations of each participant in a relation must differ. The same actions are not recommended for the two participants of a relation because the roles are neither the same nor equal. They are, however, interdependent. The proper performance of these virtues depends on both participants in a relation; ideally, one side cannot behave properly unless the other does also.

The passage continues with Mencius' use of his view of the historical development of civilization to justify the separation of rulers and farmers. He stresses how vast the class difference is and how great the sage rulers were, comparable to *tian* (social conditions, forces, the sky). Yao's and Shun's concerns were for the empire and for the people, whereas those concerned about their small plots are just farmers (*nongfu* 農夫).

Mencius then applies this theme of a vast divide based on fundamental differences of concern to another opposing dichotomy, his own (Chinese) culture, the Xia, and that of the barbarians, the Yi. He claims to have heard of being transformed from barbarian to Xia, or civilized, ways, but not vice versa. But that is what Chen Xiang is doing. Although Chen Xiang's earlier teacher, Chen Liang, was originally from the uncivilized south, the state of Chu, he learned the northern (civilized) learning of the former sages. Now, Chen Xiang is changing from Chen Liang's northern teachings back to the agrarian teachings of Xu Xing. Chen Xiang is following someone who is a barbarian from the south speaking an unintelligible language and who opposes the cultural-political way of the former kings. He is certainly not like Zengzi, who would not follow another teacher even long after Confucius had died.

By linking a person's practices with those of the barbarians, as he does here, Mencius adds deprecation to his argumentation. He continues this approach by bringing in one more set of associations. In a claim similar to the one just made, he says he has heard of birds' flying up from a dark ravine and lighting on tall trees, but not of descending from tall trees and entering a dark ravine. These images are more obviously gendered than the previous ones. Darkness and ravines, which are low lying and may be secluded, wet, and full of thick vegetation, are symbolic of women and female behavior, while trees and height are symbolic of males.

In reviewing the three main stages in Mencius' position, we can see how gender plays an important role in his argumentation. Arguing for a division of labor between the ruler and the farmers (the ruled), Mencius initially appeals to practical issues. It is simply impossible to make and grow everything that one uses. Next, he appeals to history with an account of the development of civilization. Important here is the integration of the people (farmers) into the social order of the elite from a wild (animal-like) state. Finally, Mencius appeals to certain cultural beliefs that reflect what is simply assumed about the world. These beliefs appear in the form of opposing pairs, with one side having higher value than the other.

Two clusters of contrasting associations are established. The first and superior cluster includes Mencius' northern, Confucian teachings; the way of the former sage kings; the way of Xia; a division of labor and class with the great men governing the inferior men (farmers, artisans, merchants); farming specifically with the five grains; the (patriarchal) social distinctions of the five relations; and tall trees. The inferior cluster includes no strict division of labor, so that the ruler may also farm and cook his own food (women's work); weaving (women's work) done by men; southern areas beyond the border such as the Chu state; agrarian teachings; barbarians; unintelligible languages; dark ravines; the naturally flourishing and wild conditions of the land and vegetation, the waters of rivers and marshes, animals, birds, and the people (as distinct from the rulers). Height and hills are associated with a benevolent ruler and, as seen in 4A1, Mencius objects to an inhumane ruler's occupying the high position.

From the perspective of the text's values, men are, or should be, associated with an order based on clear distinctions, which apply to governing, social relations, farming, other occupations, and environmental mastery. These associations are self-designated and pertain to masculine behavior. With the exception of those wifely activities (like weaving and cooking) that reflect their role in the social order, women are associated with a lack of those very distinctions that make for proper order. Women are metonymic with such things as wild nature, the mixing of kinds of work, the south, and barbarians. Women's maternal practices are concerned with living things whose flourishing cannot be entirely controlled, and women are themselves understood in this way. Thus things that are linked to this latter set of associations are a constant potential threat to patriarchal order, and they entail ideas about an "other."

Passage 3A4 concludes with an attempt by Chen Xiang to defend his and Xu Xing's position that denies the ruler an exemption from farming and meal preparation. Turning to the marketplace, he frames the issue in terms of sameness (*tong* 同) and difference.[9] Chen argues that cloth and silk of the same length, hemp, flax, and raw silk of the same weight, the same amounts of the five grains, and shoes of the same length all should have the same price. If they do, even a small boy will not be cheated in the marketplace. In contrast, Mencius argues that things are naturally different (*buqi* 不齊). If you try to make everything the same and deny distinctions, you bring disorder to the empire and promote dishonesty. If a big shoe and a little shoe sell for the same price, no one will make a big shoe.

Mencius changes the argument here in a slight but important way. He focuses on the differing characteristics of individual things in a given social category. Thus, shoes for example differ in their particular characteristics but all belong to the category shoe. From this viewpoint, Mencius then claims that Chen's position assumes that everything in a category can be considered similar or equivalent and that Chen is ignoring differences. Thus, Chen's position amounts to considering a big shoe and a little shoe as equivalent because they are both shoes. Mencius, however, distorts Chen's view. Chen focuses on things in a category that are similar, for instance, silk bolts of the same length and quality, not all bolts.

Mencius is implicitly drawing an analogy between shoes and men (great men and commoners, or small men). Even if they are all men, their differences matter, just as with shoes. Great men and commoners are not the same (*buqi*) and distinctions must be maintained to keep social-political order.[10] In Mencius' view, the masculinity of the gentlemen is of higher value than that of the commoners.

Chen, however, rejects the validity of the Mencian social ontology and its hierarchical order. Chen has a different conception of masculinity and the kinds of male behavior that are most valued. For Chen, the activities of men who govern are not more valuable than the activities of those who farm, cook, weave, and make implements, and indeed rulers should also engage in those activities too.

Looking at this passage in terms of gender, we see that the examples used by Chen are especially associated with women's activities, that is, making clothes, spinning, weaving, and cooking, as well as with farming, which is transcoded with maternal practices. The young boy who goes to market is associated with women, for women are the ones who take care of the children. From the Mencian viewpoint, Chen and Xu's position of refusing to accept the Mencian hierarchy and its distinctions is associated with chaos, women, others, and outsiders. For Chen and Xu, however, masculine behavior does not require the Mencian distinctions in terms of work and hierarchy. For them, masculinity is not affected if men do the same work as women, and higher class men the same as lower class men. For Mencius, it is affected. Such a blurring of boundaries is intolerable for the great men, and it only characterizes men who are the commoners, or the governed.

Thus we see how characteristics of gender are critical aspects of these specific Mencian ideas, the argumentation, and the social ontology that shapes the Mencian perspective overall. From a theoretical viewpoint, in face of the constant threat of chaos in some form, the establishment of distinctions and boundaries is part of what gender means, especially some masculine forms. Although the complexities of the Mencian position concerning gender are more fully explored in the following pages, this introductory analysis suggests that much can be recovered.

Chapter 4

Against King Hui's Self-Centered Masculinity

The behavior of men like King Hui of Liang poses a different kind of threat to Mencius' conception of social order from that of Shen Nong's followers. It is a more immediate issue in the sense that Mencius considers all the current rulers as similar to King Hui in their behavior and the institutions they have constructed. Mencius rejects King Hui's self-centered masculinity because it denies the importance of particular personal relations within the family and the political arena. Such denial leads to wrong views about the ruler and the people that in turn result in disastrous social and political actions. Mencius opposes behavior that does not promote the proper distinctions in the most fundamental patriarchal relations of ruler and minister (or ruler and vassals) and father and son.

Before we examine Mencius' specific arguments against this form of masculinity, we need to review briefly some of the assumptions that lead Mencius to oppose the model that King Hui represents. Of particular importance is Mencius' emphasis on the relational nature of personal identities. To be sure, Mencius was not alone in assuming the contextual basis of a person's identity and of a relation's characteristics. Many Chinese philosophers agreed, even if the rulers did not. To help clarify the issues, the following discussion is divided into three sections, which examine in turn the question of how identities are constructed, the behavior of the self-centered man, and conceptions of the people.

Personal Identities As Relational

Efforts to redefine governmental practices and the personal character (or behavior) of those involved in ruling are central to the Mencian teachings that focus on the notion of a benevolent government. The proposals of Mencius entail a variety of changes, particularly in the conceptions of the ruler and of the people, their relations, and relations among the elite men themselves. Mencian thought assumes that practices help to construct the identities of classes and persons and that these identities in turn lead to certain practices. Thus, the reinvention of the ruler and governmental practices entails a reinvention both of the people and of the relationship between the people and the ruler. As new practices in behavior bring changes to the conceptions of ruler and ruled, new kinds of behavior by the government are required.

These assumptions are explicit in the text. In the course of advocating his moral form of male gendered behavior, Mencius maintains that the conceptions of those who form a pair in a social relation are inseparable from the characteristics of their interaction. The ruler and the people and the characteristics of their relation constitute one example, and thus Mencius is troubled by a ruler whose behavior focuses on himself without consideration of others. Mencius also indicates that the subject (and superior) position begins the process of establishing a context and does so by how he views and treats "the other," while the position of the other (a receptive position) contributes by responding in certain ways, thus setting up an interdependent and continuing process.

A few examples will demonstrate how the text presents these ideas. In a reference to one of the five relations, Mencius claims that if a ruler were to regard his ministers as important to him as his hands and feet, they would in turn regard him as their belly and heart; if he were to regard them as dogs and horses, they would regard him as a stranger; and if he were to regard them as dirt and weeds, they would regard him as an enemy (4B3).[1] Said another way, the ministers' behavior toward the ruler is like an echo, with its quality depending on the original tone.[2] The response of the ministers depends on whether the ruler treats them as valued and personal parts of himself, or as different kinds of things of lesser value and to which the five relations do not apply, or as inferiors, possibly worthless objects to be ignored or exterminated. Not only does this passage (4B3) indicate who initiates action, and who responds accordingly, it also makes clear how relations are constructed. As the contextual analogy shifts from the closeness of the body, to the distance of domestic animals, and then to things that are objectionable, both the kinds of interaction and the identities of the two entities change. It is up to the ruler, however, as the one in the subject position, to initiate action.

In another example Mencius says that to give food to a gentleman but not be kind (*ai* 愛) to him is to treat him as a pig (7A37). To be kind to him but not respect (*jing* 敬) him is to treat him as a domestic animal. While this passage goes on to stress that the ruler's respect must not be false, the idea is clear here too that how one conceives the other in a relational pair is inseparable from how one treats that other, and how one treats the other reflects how one conceives of oneself, especially in relation to that other.

A further example of the relational and contextual aspect of identities occurs in one of the original interviews and applies to the ruler and the people (1B12). Here Mencius gives the advice that a true king should not hoard food and keep his granaries full in times of famine, for if he does, the old and weak will die in the ditches and the strong young men will scatter in all directions. In such a situation, the people will then not come to the aid of officers in battle but instead will just watch them die. If the ruler practices benevolent government, however, his people will treat their superiors affectionately as parents (*qinqishang* 親其上) and will even die for their elders (*siqizhang* 死其長). Thus, if the king conceives himself to be like a benevolent parent and behaves accordingly, the people will respond like grateful children. On the other hand, his callousness to them will result in their exhibiting indifferent and hostile behavior to him.

Elsewhere in the text Mencius speaks about the inseparability of context, behavior, and type of relation by noting that nobility, age, and virtue are three things respected by everyone and that virtue is best for aiding the world and ruling the people (2B2). That is, while behavior based on distinctions of rank applies to the context of noblemen's practices at court and behavior based on distinctions of age applies to the context of villagers' practices, moral behavior applies to the new family-like political context of the ruler's practices in governing the people.

Mencius is also trying to change the behavior and conception of friends, one of the five relations, as well as the ruler and the people. Thus he claims that the relation of friendship should have a moral basis (*de* 德) and should not be a matter of political alliances (5B3). Meng Xian serves as his first example. The head of a large family, Meng Xian was a great nobleman who had five friends, all without the same level of political power and connections that he had. Mencius claims that if these five men had become friendly with Meng Xian because of his powerful family, Meng Xian would not have maintained a friendship with them. Meng Xian could be a friend with them because they paid no attention to his position. That is, their friendship was based on virtue, not on such political criteria as rank and power. Duke Hui of Bi behaved similarly, even though he was the ruler of a small state and thus even more powerful than Meng Xian. Hui said that he treated Zisi as his teacher, Yan Ban as his friend, and Wang Shun and Chang Xi as vassals serving him. Here we see how behavior helps define a relationship, no matter whether one is a nobleman, a ruler, a gentleman, or sage emperor.

Mencius gives two additional examples in this passage to emphasize the inclusiveness of his view that moral behavior, not rank, should be the basis for the relation of friends. When the virtuous Duke Ping of Jin visited Hai Tang, a virtuous recluse, Hai Tang entertained the duke in accordance with the duke's virtue, not in accordance with his higher position as ruler of a large state. And, the sage emperor Yao treated the virtuous Shun with great respect, even though the latter was his son-in-law and supposedly a commoner.[3] Mencius claims that the moral obligation is the same, whether it is an inferior's showing respect to a superior (honoring those with rank, *guigui* 貴貴) or a superior's showing respect to an inferior (honoring the virtuous, *zunxian* 尊賢). Scholars usually point out that the latter situation challenges customary practices by making wisdom and virtue as important as rank, but we also need to keep in mind how the behavior itself of showing respect helps to alter the conception of the initiator and recipient of that behavior.

Mencius speaks further about these interrelationships as he employs the concepts of *xing* (natural tendencies, propensities, dispositions) and *ming* 命 (social-moral circumstances, surrounding conditions). He says that the preference of the mouth for good tastes, the eyes for beautiful appearances, the ears for harmonious sounds, the nose for fragrant odors, and the four limbs for peaceful resting is a matter of one's natural tendencies (*xing*), but since social-moral circumstances (*ming*) are involved too, the gentleman does not say that these sensory pursuits are just of matter of one's natural tendencies (7B24). Exhibiting benevolence in the father and son relation, appropriateness in the ruler and minister relation, ritual propriety in the guest and host (*binzhu* 賓主) relation, wisdom among virtuous men (*xianzhe* 賢者), and sageliness in regard to the ways of the surrounding conditions (*tiandao* 天道) are matters of behaving according to social-moral circumstances, but since one's natural tendencies are involved too, the gentleman does not say they are only matters of circumstances. Reflecting its later textual layer, this passage expands the four virtues to five and employs the concept of *xing*. The *xing* aspect refers to the fact that one is able to do something in a biological sense, while the *ming* aspect refers to the social-moral context and conditions. That an adult son should defer to his father is a matter of *ming*, a social and moral matter, but he also needs to eat, a matter of *xing*, a biological matter. How he actually behaves reveals his conception of his father, himself, and their relationship.

These examples from *Mencius* are just a few that illustrate and support his view that the behavior of the two parties in a relation constructs that relation as well as the personal identities of each party. The broader context is critical too. Although the text contains many other examples, I have cited here some that pertain to the relation of ruler and minister and of friend and friend from among the five relations and the relation of the ruler and the people, a relation of special importance to Mencius.

Rejecting Self-Centered Behavior

Given the above understanding of how the behavior of rulers and elite men help establish the relations that make up social and political order, we can understand the reasons that Mencius argues against both the agrarian and self-centered forms of masculinity.[4] Mencius refers to the latter as inhumane (*buren* 不仁), and he portrays and attacks the inhumane ruler's behavior in a variety of ways. Unlike those who embody the agrarian position and whose behavior evokes unwanted associations with the feminine behavior of feeding, the inhumane ruler accepts hierarchical distinctions of class, he focuses on matters that affect the empire, and his behavior is not considered tainted by feminine associations. However, he ignores the distinctions of personal family relations, which Mencius considers essential. This characteristic leads Mencius to reject this form of male behavior because paradoxically it is not infused with certain (other) feminine traits, especially those associated with maternal behavior.

In some passages Mencius mentions undesirable characteristics that a particular ruler has, while in others he focuses on desirable characteristics that a ruler lacks. Mencius often uses the term *buren*, which may be translated as inhumane, ruthless, cruel, or not benevolent. In some cases Mencius refers to specific actions and attitudes, while in others he uses general descriptive terms. His criticism is wide-ranging and plentiful but is not as finely argued as is his opposition to agrarian masculinity. Mencius' arguments against undesirable characteristics here are often based on pragmatic reasoning as he stresses the consequences of the ruler's actions. At the same time, his arguments for new kinds of royal behavior incorporate both pragmatic reasoning and a type of foundational reasoning that appeals to inborn traits. Scattered throughout the text, his comments fall under topics that especially function within social contexts of men. These topics consist of political goals, treatment of the people, military matters, administrative matters, and personal character. The following discussion indicates how Mencius' conception of the inhumane ruler also implies a specific conception of the people and the ruler's relation to them.

This type of ruler is primarily interested in his own power and wealth and ignores the relevance of personal relations within the family and empire. He behaves according to a standard of personal benefit and profit (*li* 利), which Mencius opposes to his own sagely standard of moral behavior. For Mencius, the latter includes benevolence and rightness (*renyi*), kindness (*en* 恩), protecting and nurturing (*bao*), treating the old and young appropriately (*laowulao* 老吾老, *youwuyou* 幼吾幼), maintaining unwavering moral feelings (*hengxin* 恆心), holding on to the fundamentals (*ben* 本), and exhibiting respectful, thrifty, courteous, and humble behavior (*gong* 恭, *jian* 儉, *li* 禮, *xia* 下). This scale of masculine behavior is commonly phrased as *li* (selfish benefit) versus *yi* (rightness) and is seen as having a self-oriented and nonrelational focus at one end and an other-oriented and relational focus at the other end. Also correlated with the *li-yi* scale is a separate and different scale that opposes force or strength (*li* 力) and virtue (*de*), or physical strength and moral strength. As the above concepts suggest, the relational kinds of behavior summarized in the term *yi* are closely and openly associated with female gendered behavior. Moreover, with the exception of benevolence and rightness, which are used throughout the text, those listed above appear only in the later textual layers, thus suggesting amplification of Mencius' views.[5]

Treating King Hui of Liang as the epitome of this self-centered behavior, Mencius lays out the stark contrast between the king's type of masculinity and what he Mencius advocates. Conceiving these two forms of behavior as not merely different but in strong conflict, Mencius claims that a man cannot both practice benevolence and rightness and pursue personal benefit (1A1), or practice benevolence and strive for wealth (3A3). The reason is that benevolence and rightness respectively mean a man's taking care of his father and a man's deferring to his ruler (1A1), whereas the pursuit of personal profit and benefit entails not recognizing the relations of father and son and of ruler and minister since it rejects benevolence and rightness.[6] Mencius adds that actions done for profit especially injure these relations and will eventually lead to the destruction of one's family and state.

Mencius emphasizes this message in a later conversation about King Hui, whose behavior resulted in great harm to his family and state (7B1). Here, Mencius describes a benevolent man as one who broadens his concern from those he loves (*ai*) to those he does not love, that is, from those within his own family to those beyond it, and an inhumane man as one who does the reverse. That is, he broadens his "outside" behavior pertaining to those he does not love to those "inside" whom he loves. Wanting to increase his personal profit by expanding his territory, King Hui waged a war that ended in defeat and mass destruction of his people. To avoid defeat a second time, he sent to war even those whom he loved, namely, his sons and younger brothers, but they also were killed. Mencius' point is that self-centered behavior (embodied here in the search for profit) will destroy the relations of father and son and older and younger brother, as well as the people themselves, because it ignores the critical importance of these relations. This view is supported in a further passage, in which Mencius claims that a ruler who lets go of the moral way has few supporters, and even his own relatives may rebel against him (2B1).

While it fundamentally implies a denial of relationships, inhumane behavior has a range of possible emphases, from uncaring and indifferent behavior to that which is actively ruthless and cruel. An inhumane ruler may be kind to his animals, for instance, but he is not kind to the people and he does not protect them (1A7). Mencius is not saying that such a ruler is always intentionally cruel. Instead, the ruler's concern with his own wealth and power is so great that he simply does not see and so does not care about the consequences of his actions, especially human suffering. Most important, he does not make the effort to be kind (1A7). The ruler's indifference to others turns into cruelty, however, as soon as he recognizes that he could relieve the people's suffering but does not.

Uncaring and indifferent to others, such a ruler treats the people harshly (1A3). He is fond of war and likes to kill (1A3, 1A6), and he does not share either the economic necessities of life or his pleasures with the people. Thus their conditions are desperate, and many starve and are abandoned (1B1, 1B12). Passages from the later textual layers add details to these descriptions and emphasize the disastrous results of the ruler's unconcerned attitude toward the people and his treatment of others.

King Hui's type of government, like his character, is also described as unfeeling and cruel (2A1). Such a ruler uses force but disguises it as benevolence to subdue people, and so they never truly submit in their hearts (2A3). He feeds his own animals and keeps extra food in his granaries while the people starve to death and their families become separated (1A4). He taxes the people heavily, entraps and drowns them, punishes them harshly, interferes with the timing of their farming activities, and allows the boundaries of the fields to become unclear, a situation reflecting a despotic ruler and corrupt officials (1A5, 1A7, 3A3). In other words, he does not properly manage the people's livelihood. By being called to war or corvee labor, the people are prevented from doing their seasonal work in a timely fashion, and so they suffer hardships of hunger, cold, separation from family, and death (1A3, 1A5). He destroys the people's houses to make ponds and turns their fields into parks, so that the people have no place to live and farm. He lets the empire become chaotic with animals roaming about, and he allows heresies and violence to flourish among the elite (1A4, 3B9). He even offends the great aristocratic families (4A6).

In taxing, he does not take into consideration how good or bad the harvest is. He taxes too much in bad years, so that the people cannot properly take care of their fathers and mothers and they end up abandoning their old and young in the ditches (1A7, 3A3). He may tax so much so that some of the people die from starvation, and when he taxes even more, fathers and sons become separated, resulting in the breakup of families (7B27). Taxation that is too heavy causes merchants as well as farmers to suffer (2A5). In some cases, however, he reduces taxes too much, so that he cannot maintain all the distinctions that are needed for civilization (6B10).

Mencius claims that all the current rulers are inhumane because they all love to kill (1A6). Moreover, the elites as well as the people suffer. By starting wars, such a ruler puts his officials in danger and incurs the hatred of the feudal lords. His ambitions are blatantly those of domination; he wants to increase the size of his territory, force other states to pay him homage, and in general rule over the other states and the barbarians (1A7). In attacking another state, he kills their fathers and older brothers, captures their sons and younger brothers, destroys their ancestral temples, and takes their valuable ritual vessels (1B11). (Note that these actions indicate the critical importance of the patriarchal relations and their symbolic objects.) In addition, an inhumane ruler is corrupt, disrespectful, and shortsighted in administrative matters, for he appoints ministers who are untrustworthy and without ability (1B7). Mencius sharply contrasts the inhumane ruler to a true king, who will not do these things if he takes over another state and is welcomed by the people.

The self-centered behavior of an uncaring ruler applies both to his person and his governmental actions. He spreads evil among the people just as a benevolent ruler practices benevolence (4A1), and his lack of morality leads to disorder at all levels of government and society. Those among the elite, for example, do not conform to the codes or do their duties, while those below engage in criminal behavior. The behavior of such a ruler inverts orderly processes and accepted ways of thinking to the extent that dangers become seen as a way to bring peace, disasters as a way to bring benefits, and lethal activities as a cause for pleasure (4A8). Mencius describes current feudal lords in similar ways, pointing out how their self-centered behavior affects family members, men in government, and those who are weak and vulnerable. They violate or ignore the injunctions of former leaders that are necessary for political order (6B7).[7]

Implicit of course in Mencius' depictions of an inhumane ruler is a set of ideals that a ruler should embody in his behavior. These ideals make for a benevolent ruler and true king, one depicted as father and mother of the people. The inhumane ruler has none of the compassion and other-directed behavior associated with mothers in this phrase. Although the inhumane ruler recognizes patriarchal social distinctions in terms of occupational class, he ignores social distinctions that concern personal relations. He does not consider his personal identity to be based on a web of relations with others, and he uses force instead of benevolence. Thus Mencius argues against this widespread form of masculine behavior that has clearly demonstrated its destructive consequences.

Conceptions of the People

Mencius is interested in the behavior of the ruler because it affects the lives of the people, who are his ultimate concern. The people are conceived collectively, as a social group distinct from the ruler and others in the ruling elite. The people do not share in governing and are often used by rulers for their own purposes. The people are thought of as below, while the rulers, officials, and gentlemen are above. Despite the great gradations in rank and power among those within the ruling elite, the less powerful and lower ranked are still not part of the people. There is a vast divide between the (noble) men and the people.

While most thinkers, but not those following the agrarian position, agree that the people are "other" in some way, their characteristics as a social group are a matter of dispute. Not surprisingly, the conception of the people is dependent upon the conception of the ruler. References that indicate the presumed characteristics of the people are found in the midst of Mencius' conversations with rulers and others, but the purpose of these conversations is not to examine characteristics of the people or ever address them directly. Rather, Mencius is concerned with advising the ruler on what to do, given his ambitions and the people's traits. Mencius often offers his ideas by using analogies and images that are intended to provoke the ruler to change his outlook and begin to understand the political situation from his (Mencius') perspective. The images used to refer to the people are well known and culturally powerful, and the particular ones selected are of course critical. One analogy can result in one set of characteristics, while another can yield quite different ones. Similar traits drawn from different images and different traits drawn from the same image can lead to differing evaluations of the people's characteristics. This issue is important because the ruler's behavior toward the people, or at least his justification of his behavior, is closely tied to his evaluations of their characteristics in addition to his own desires and self-conception.

The people are directly compared to oxen and sheep (2B4) and (domestic) animals (3A4), and they are indirectly compared to arable land that has not been clearly divided into distinct fields (3A3). The image of water rushing downward after a heavy rain is also one that is used (1A6). Oxen, sheep, and animals are all considered as naturally lacking self-control, self-regulation, and a sense of how to order their lives collectively as a group. They are believed to have no group morality but instead to focus on their own individual desires. Behaving as separate entities, they have no social ordering characteristics comparable to the five relations of the ruling elite. Land that is uncultivated or has improperly demarcated boundaries is similar in that it too has no natural distinctions that provide order. As an undifferentiated mass, it is inherently disorderly. The people are considered similar insofar as they lack distinctions and norms that would provide social order for the group.

Mencius and inhumane rulers draw different conclusions from these characteristics, and so they differ in their answers to how a ruler should behave. Assuming that the people can be used like animals and land to satisfy the ruler's aims, an inhumane ruler is indifferent to whatever feelings the people may have. He controls both the people and his animals, but having a closer daily relation to his own domestic animals, he may even treat them better than the people. Consequently, the people's lives are filled with misery.

Mencius alludes to this situation when he compares a ruler with someone charged with taking care of another person's oxen and sheep (2B4). A substitute shepherd would try to find enough food for the animals, and if he could not, he would return them to their owner. He would not simply let them die from starvation. An inhumane ruler does just that, however. In years of a bad harvest and famine, he just lets the old and weak people fall into the ditches (and die) and lets the strong young men scatter in all directions, thus destroying families.

The shepherd analogy suggests that rulers take care of, and keep in order, living things that differ from men in not having group order. Just as a shepherd oversees flocks or herds of animals, the ruler oversees the flock of the people. What then is the conclusion to be drawn? Do the people exist only to serve the purposes of the ruler? Should the ruler use the people for his own ends, just as the shepherd eventually sells the animals to be killed and eaten? The behavior of an inhumane ruler indicates that his answer is yes.

Mencius disagrees. Mencius' views are the subject of the remaining chapters in this study and so will not be addressed here except in regard to a few brief points. While he assumes that the people are different from the men or ruling elite, he does believe they have some characteristics in common, especially the abilities to learn and to contribute to political order by maintaining social distinctions. This view is partly the reason he says that benevolent government must begin with marking the boundaries of the fields. Agricultural boundaries are analogous to social distinctions, and both are deemed necessary to bring order to that which is inherently without order. Although the processes are different for the people and the land, establishing distinctions can be done in both cases. When achieved successfully, both kinds of distinctions contribute to social well-being.

Mencius agrees that the people inherently lack social distinctions, but he disagrees with the implications of the image of the shepherd and his flock that is accepted by the inhumane ruler. Mencius offers another analogy that also characterizes the people as formless but carries positive associations. He suggests that the people are like water rushing down after a rain, bringing renewed life to the young plants. If the ruler wants to pacify and unite the empire, he should get rid of his fondness for killing. The people will then rush to him like water flowing downward and will give new life to his state just as water enables plants to grow. Despite their natural formlessness, the people are the source of political life just as water is for biological life.

Thus we see that even though Mencius agrees with the inhumane rulers that the people inherently lack the social distinctions that provide collective order, the different analogies used in conceiving the people lead to different conclusions about how the ruler should behave. For the uncaring ruler, the people's lack of internal ordering justifies his forceful use of them for his own ends. For Mencius, however, it means that the ruler should change his destructive ways and recognize that the people are part of the necessary foundation of all states. They are more like water than like oxen or sheep. Moreover, they are like the life giving water of timely rain, not the water of floods that destroys fields and lives.

Chapter 5

Compassionate Governing
Dynamics, References, and Practices

The proposed benevolent government of Mencius involves changes in governmental practices and in the personal character of the ruler himself. Governmental practices are directed primarily toward the people, but some efforts are directed toward others in the ruling elite, inside or outside government. The personal cultivation of the ruler as a moral-social person in accordance with the five relations entails two contexts, his family and the empire. In terms of social relations and personal qualities, Mencian ideas introduce new conceptions of the ruler, the people, and their relationship. Governmental practices are discussed in this chapter and the ruler's character in the following two chapters. In this examination of the new practices that characterize the Mencian benevolent government, a primary question is how these masculine practices reflect transformations of some maternal practices. To help answer this question, we shall consider some dynamics of personal behavior, specific terms used, and the content of the proposed governmental practices.

Maternal Dynamics

The views of Mencius incorporate the kind of knowledge that one often has who occupies a subordinate position within a social-political system. Such a person theoretically has no real political power and yet can wield enormous influence as a result of relationships of affection and use of moral power. This person is a specific type of female, a wife who is also a mother. As a wife she is inferior to her husband, and so the primary way she can gain power of her own is to establish, and behave within, a separate system of authority. I think of it as functioning in a way somewhat comparable to the Han development of the canon as a scriptural authority that shared power with the political, imperial authority. With Mencius, this other system is a maternal familial system. Because of specific requirements relating to the concern with life, successful maternal dynamics rely on feelings of affection and on moral power, not brute force. They are effective because they are based in certain "natural" capacities of human beings, including their feelings, needs, and desires.

By comparing the political context that Mencius advocates with a maternal context, we see how the actions of a benevolent ruler are similar to those necessary for a mother toward her child, and the actions of a cruel ruler lead to the destruction of children. That is, the mother must provide the child with the necessities of life such as food and water and protection, she must teach, lead, and guide the child as he or she grows, she must be kind and loving if the child is to develop in a healthy and social way, she must share pleasures with the child for feelings of happiness or joy are a part of becoming a healthy human being, and she must be an emotional home for the child. If the mother does these things well, the child will presumably grow to be loving and compliant in return.

The dynamics are critical. Ideally, the mother's "gifts" to her children result in their developing feelings of love, gratefulness, and indebtedness. Such feelings then lead a son, as an adult, to reproduce his mother's earlier behavior toward him by his taking good care of her in her old age. A daughter will repeat the maternal pattern in actuality, and she will also express her indebtedness through her behavior to her husband's parents. The moral power of the mother is gained from her compassionate actions toward the young and weak child when she (the mother) is in the position of strength in relation to the child. When her tacit teachings of the dynamics of moral power are effective, the stronger and more powerful treat the weaker in a kind way.

It may appear that the stronger behave in a kind way voluntarily, but the motivations are deeply and unconsciously embodied in the character of a person, in the feelings and sensibilities that a person has developed. Thus, even if it seems to be at great cost, the stronger feels compelled to behave compassionately toward the weaker. Such compassionate behavior then elicits in the weaker, and reinscribes in the stronger, those familiar feelings and actions of love, gratefulness, and indebtedness once felt toward one's mother. A Mencian insight is that the person who gives attains a position of power and morality, while those who receive occupy the weak position. In advocating governmental practices that offer the gift of compassion, Mencian thought is employing the model of ideal maternal practices.

While advocating hierarchical and patriarchal distinctions as a way to promote order, Mencius also makes feelings critical to his position. The advocacy of feelings, specifically pleasure and pain, works theoretically to evoke the maternal context within which these feelings originally developed and functioned. The maternal context is thus concurrent with the patriarchal context and serves as a tacit source of ideas for Mencius. That is, Mencian ideas function politically within the context of patriarchal order, but philosophically they implicitly appropriate aspects of the maternal context, which is not an openly recognized aspect of the patriarchal order of the five relations.

Terms and Concepts

There is no single term used for the proposed benevolent practices of a ruler. Some terms are more specific and others more abstract as they reflect differing emphases. Focusing on ruling practices as opposed to the role or the person of ruler, the original interviews of Mencius use the terms *wangdao* 王道, the royal way, the way to rule as a true king (1A3); *shirenzhengyumin* 施仁政於民, extend benevolent government to the people (1A5); *wang* 王, royal government, to rule in a royal way, to be a (true) king (1A5, 1B1); and *xingrenzheng* 行仁政, practice benevolent government (1B12).

Passages from later textual layers also employ the term *wang* (in 1A7 and many other passages), while introducing other similar terms that generally highlight some aspect of the conditions of benevolent government. Referring to the benevolent ruler himself or characteristics of his governmental practices and appearing only in later textual layers, these terms and phrases include *wangzhe* 王者, one who rules in a royal way, one who is a true king (1A3); *fazhengshiren* 發政施仁, in governing extend benevolence (1A7); *dedaozhe* 得道者, one who has attained the moral way (2B1), *renhe* 人和, the harmony of (the) men (2B1); *zhiminzhichan* 制民之產, regulate the production (livelihood) of the people (1A7); *baomin* 保民, protect and love the people (1A7); *yongen* 用恩, employ kindness (1A7); and *tuien* 推恩, extend kindness (1A7). Also appearing only later are the familial and moral terms: *weiminfumu* 為民父母, father and mother of the people (1A4, 1B7, 3A3); *laowulao, youwuyou*, treat one's own aged properly, treat one's own young properly (1A7); *fumu* 父母, father and mother (2A5); *fumuzhixin* 父母之心, heart (feelings) of a father and mother (3B3); *xianjun* 賢君, virtuous ruler (3A3); *xianzhe*, one who is virtuous (1A2); and *renrenzaiwei* 仁人在位, a benevolent man in the (ruling) position (3A3).

Many of these terms explicitly or implicitly evoke women as mothers and the compassionate feelings and love associated with them.

In addition to these kinds of references to benevolent governmental practices, Mencius uses contrasting concepts to highlight differences in methods of governing. For example, virtue (*de*) is opposed to force (*li*), with the claim that a ruler practices actual benevolence (*ren*) if he employs virtue, but he only imitates benevolence if he uses force (2A3). Those who submit to a ruler because of his force do not submit in their hearts. If they submit because of the ruler's virtue, however, they are pleased in their hearts (*zhongxinyue* 中心悅) and they genuinely submit. The historical examples of Kings Tang and Wen are cited as support here. Thus virtue, the heart, pleasure, what is genuine, benevolence, King Wen, and Tang are linked together and opposed to physical force. Virtue, benevolence, and force are abstractions here that summarize the specific governmental practices that Mencius discusses in detail elsewhere.

The fact that the people (*min*, adult males) are often specifically mentioned as the recipient of the proposed governmental policies makes the class and gender dimension clear from the language itself. And, even when the people are not literally mentioned, as in such examples as *wang* or *xingrenzheng*, the content of the ideas confirms that the conception of kingly rule entails ruling practices that are aimed mostly at the people, not at the elite. The exceptions belong to the later layers of the text, where officials and other elite men are more noticeably subjects of concern, thus suggesting changes in political conditions.

Practices Regarding the People

As seen in the previous chapter, Mencius claims that a true king will care about benevolence and rightness, but not about profit to himself or his state, for profit comes at the expense of others, ultimately destroying self and others (1A1, 7B1). Although this statement appears to be unambiguous, the particular actions to which the abstractions of benevolence and rightness refer are actually not at all obvious. The implication of these ideas is that they in effect advocate that the ruler expand to the people in a limited way certain opportunities (supposedly) already enjoyed by the ruling elite class. A true king will thus implement practices that will enable the people also to experience conditions of sufficient food, adequate shelter, pleasures, intact families, and sufficient resources for proper social and ritual behavior.[1]

Looking first at the original Mencius interviews and as noted previously, we see that the people's activities include cultivating grain, catching fish and turtles, cutting wood, and being subject to conscription in the king's army and labor projects (1A3). Mencius claims that the people will have plenty of food and fuel if the king does not interfere with the farmers' seasonal work by demands for corvee labor or military service, does not allow nets that are too finely-meshed, and does not allow the people into the mountain forests except during certain times of year. And if this happens, the people will be able to nourish their living and mourn their dead without having any regrets (*yangshengsangsiwuhan* 養生喪死無憾).

Mencius continues with the claim that enabling the people to nourish their living and mourn their dead without regrets is the beginning of the kingly way (*wangdao*), or compassionate government. Although this statement is often understood in a rather general way, it has specific references. Given the historical and social contexts, nourishing and mourning refer to ritual practices, not just general acts of kindness and concern. Such ritual practices help to construct a certain type of social order, and both are essential to the kingly way. A later passage, 3A2, makes it explicit that the ritual actions of nourishing and mourning refer to a son's properly taking care of his parents in life and in death and that such behavior is termed filial (*xiao*).[2]

The ruler must do more than just manage and regulate the conditions of the people's livelihood. According to Mencius, a true king provides food for the people in times of famine and bad harvests (1B12). This idea is reinforced in later passages, for instance, in 2A1, where Mencius claims that practicing benevolent government is easy and can be done by the ruler's ensuring that the hungry and thirsty have enough to eat and drink. In other words, a true king feeds the people, just as a mother feeds her infant.

Another original conversation (1A5) provides additional details about the people's life. They are subject to punishment and taxation, they raise crops, they are encouraged to cultivate and practice the filial and fraternal virtues of filial piety, fraternal respect, loyalty, and good faith (*xiao*, *ti*, *zhong* 忠, *xin* 信), and they fight in the ruler's armies. Implicitly rejecting the desires of rulers to enlarge their territory, Mencius claims that a ruler does not need extensive territory to be a king. Rather, he can be a king with a small area if he extends benevolent government to the people by such policies as imposing only light punishments and taxes, by ensuring that the people plow their fields deeply and weed in a timely manner, and by encouraging the young men (*zhuangzhe* 壯者) to practice the above mentioned virtues, so that they may properly serve (*shi* 事) their fathers and older brothers when they are at home and their elders and superiors when they are out in the community. Mencius states that such actions will enable the population to win easily in battle against stronger states.

Other rulers engage in warfare in order to increase their territory and population and thereby their wealth and power. The Mencian position offers another way for a ruler to expand his population and so perhaps also his wealth and power, while it discounts the importance of having a large expanse of territory. Mencius recognizes that even a true king has to engage in war at times, but it is the love of killing that he rejects. Thus, Mencius maintains that if a ruler pursues his proposed path, the people of other states will look for his coming and will take refuge (*gui* 歸) in him like water flowing downward (1A6).[3] Moreover, this kind of ruler will take over another state only if it pleases the people, who indeed will welcome such a ruler to their state (1B10, 1B11, 3B5). By insisting that a true king considers the people more important than the territory and would even abandon the land if he had to choose between it and the people, Mencius is following the model of ancestral Zhou leaders mentioned in the *Odes* (1B15).

The Mencian opposition to a love of militarism is part of his policy of "returning to the root." Not appearing in the earliest textual layers, the term root takes on added meanings between the middle and later layers of the text. In 1A7, the root refers to economic and educational policies, whereas later it refers to the gentleman's heart or feelings and inborn moral dispositions (7A21), a shift toward more clear maternal associations. If the ruler returns to the root and so governs by extending benevolence (*fazhengshiren*, 1A7), then all types of people will come to his state voluntarily, whether they are aspiring officers in the empire, tillers, merchants, travelers, or political dissenters. A ruler will not need to use force to be successful, for the people will easily follow him once they have a sufficient livelihood, that is, have enough to eat. Thus we see that like a mother a ruler should first ensure that the people have sufficient food, and the emphasis on feeding and its pleasures has tacit associations with maternal behavior.

The notion of planning ahead is important because it is believed to underlie social order, which distinguishes a good society from the wild state thought to be characteristic of nature and wild animals. Planning ahead is a necessary aspect of a benevolent government's policy of ensuring a steady livelihood (*hengchan* 恆產) for the people (1A7).[4] Mencius claims that without a steady livelihood the people will lack steady hearts (*hengxin*), or unwavering moral feelings, and so act recklessly, commit crimes, and consequently suffer punishments. In effect, they will act like wild animals. Such a situation is not regarded as their fault, moreover, but is considered entrapment by a ruler who has not properly managed the people's work.

Discussing benevolent government in terms of roots or fundamentals, the comments in 1A7 (a later passage) include more direct references to women as mothers and wives than the original interviews and remembered conversations do. According to this passage, a true king will ensure that the people (married men) have sufficient food and resources to serve their fathers and mothers "in looking up" and to support their wives and children (*qizi*) "in looking down." Such a king will ensure they have plenty to eat when the harvest is plentiful and not die of starvation when the harvest fails. Then, when he urges them to practice moral behavior, they will easily comply.[5]

A return to the fundamentals emphasizes the responsibilities that younger adults have toward their elders. Thus, the basics include planting mulberry trees so that fifty-year olds can wear silk; raising chickens, dogs, and pigs so that seventy-year olds can eat meat; and not conscripting farmers during the busy seasons so that the crops will be successful. Young men are to be taught how to be filial and fraternal so that the elderly, the grey-haired ones, will not have to struggle to support themselves in their old age. Only a true king will enable both the young and the old to escape from hunger and cold (1A7, 1A3). Many of these activities, including sericulture, weaving, raising domestic animals, and instruction are especially associated with the behavior of women as wives. The idea of a refuge, or place to regard as home, is also closely associated with the feelings and behavior linked to mothers.

Passages from later textual layers express similar ideas and expand on them, with King Wen often serving as the model of a benevolent ruler. Describing the conditions of King Wen's benevolent government in even more specific terms, Mencius claims, for instance, that the tillers were taxed one-ninth, the aristocratic gentlemen received hereditary salaries, there were inspections but no taxes at the border stations and markets, fish traps were not restricted in use, criminals were punished but not their wives and children, and the four most destitute kinds of people were given help first. These types were old men and women without spouses, old men who had no sons, and young boys who had no father (1B5). It is noteworthy that, in addition to indicating how a benevolent government treats the different types of people, another kind of governmental practice is mentioned here that is associated especially with King Wen, namely, taking care of those people seen as destitute because of their lack of certain social relations.

Although the particular social relations whose lack makes one destitute are only ones included in the five relations (so that a young boy or girl without a mother is not considered destitute) and apparently do not include other kinds of relations, compassion and special treatment are advocated, as opposed to an emphasis on (patriarchal) duties and moral virtues. Compassionate treatment is especially associated with mothers, moreover.

The topic of food remains critical throughout the text. For instance, the importance of the people's having a steady livelihood is again stressed in 3A3 (a late passage), in which the ideal ruler is variously referred to as a benevolent man in the position of authority (*renrenzaiwei*), a virtuous ruler (*xianjun*), father and mother of the people (*weiminfumu*), and a true king (*wangzhe*). The people's livelihood is called by a more abstract term here, *minshi*, the people's affairs, but the assumptions are similar to those in other passages. That is, since it is believed that the people will behave morally if they have reliable work and immorally if they do not, a true king will give immediate attention to their affairs.

This passage offers descriptions of a true king's behavior that seem typical of a wife's behavior and descriptions of his governmental practices that evoke associations with maternal practices.[6] For example, a true king's land and tax policies will enable adult men to take care of (*yang*) their fathers and mothers as well as the very old and very young. The duties taught in the schools will include the five relations (*renlun*), expanding from the two filial and fraternal duties as in earlier passages, and it is claimed that when the elite class above illustrates these relations, then below the "little children" people (*xiaomin*) will treat their parents properly. This passage also mentions the well-field system and the idea that benevolent government must begin with marking the boundaries of the fields. It is claimed that this action is needed to ensure a correct division of the land so that officials can receive their proper income, that is, eat.

Slightly different details and emphases appear in other later passages. For instance, in 7A22 and 4A13, King Wen, the filial son and outstanding model for a benevolent ruler, is admired because he is good at taking care of the aged (*shanyanglao* 善養老), behavior typically performed by mothers-wives within the family. Mencius states that benevolent men, that is, filial men, regard someone who is good at taking care of the aged as their refuge or home. King Wen thus partly behaves as a wife does toward her parents-in-law, but in his case he extends to the empire this female familial behavior. Mothers, home, and family are associated with *gui* (return to, take refuge in), and this association is further emphasized by Mencius' continuing remarks about practices for each family.

Mencius briefly references King Wen's military successes but pays most of his attention to the king's other actions of leadership. These include the king's regulating the division of land for fields; instructing the men in planting mulberry trees, raising animals, and tilling the land; and teaching their wives to take care of the older people. The result was there were no hungry and cold elderly among the people of King Wen. It is interesting that this last (northern) textual layer does not mention the filial and fraternal instruction of young men or a man's proper ritual behavior toward his parents while living and after death, but it does mention some sort of instruction for wives, to help them nourish the aged. In contrast to the earliest passages, this later passage (7A22) openly recognizes the presence of women, both in the kind of work a wife does and in the wife's duties to take care of her husband's parents.

A further and significant characteristic of the practices of a true king is that he shares his pleasures with the people.[7] Two examples of the king's pleasures in the original interviews are musical performances and hunting (1B1). In his argument for sharing these things, Mencius persuades the king to agree that genuine enjoyment is not achieved alone. Mencius establishes that feelings of enjoyment are part of a relationship, and he further shows that other kinds of feelings are relational too. That is, when people hear the king's music and imagine his pleasure, they are reminded of their own pain. Their suffering comes from having to endure hardships so severe that fathers and sons, and men's brothers, wives, and children become separated from one another.

Mencius stresses that feelings are especially associated with the family and those feelings are of the most fundamental kind. Indeed, family relationships and feelings are not separate; they help to construct each other. By sharing his feelings of enjoyment with the people, the kingly ruler is implicitly forming a relationship with the people that is similar to familial relationships and their shared feelings. Family, home, and feelings are especially linked to the heart and maternal compassion. Thus, emerging here in Mencius' position is not the patriarchal emphasis on distinctions, duties, and social order (as in some other passages), but a maternal kind of emphasis on feelings, family, joy, and inclusiveness. A true king's sharing his pleasures with the people is metonymic with maternal feelings, and this association also reinforces the transcoding of farming and maternal practices.

The idea of enjoyment receives attention in later passages too. Referred to as one who is virtuous (*xianzhe*), such a ruler can only enjoy his terrace and pools, birds and animals, if he shares them with the people (1A2).

Mencius indicates that it is permissible for a true king to enjoy wealth and women (*haose* 好色) if he also allows the people to have that kind of enjoyment (1B5, 1B4).[8] A true king should take pleasure in the people's pleasures and worry about the people's problems, and if he does so, they will reciprocate. People will want to live in his state and will take pleasure in following his policies (2A5). Such behavior, by the ruler and ruled, will enable the ruler to transform the governing context into a familial one, with himself as father and mother of the children-people.

The specific proposals of Mencius are all designed to contribute to the formation of a new kind of political body. Knowing that the ruler's concern differs in regard to the people and the officials, Mencius recommends such measures for the people as lightening taxes, appropriately planning and regulating the people's livelihood, educating them, and letting them share in some of the ruler's pleasures. Once the lives of the people are improved, they will also begin to behave in new ways. He claims, for instance, that they will remain in their villages, be friendly to each other, help each other in keeping guard, and aid each other during illnesses. As a result, they will be affectionate and harmonious (3A3).

Mencian governmental practices thus aim at more than simply regulating the people. Mencius aspires to motivate the ruler to conceive and treat the people as family, for he believes that then the people will begin to display familial and warm feelings toward the ruler and each other. The ways to obtain the people's genuine affection is somehow to revive those feelings of love and pleasure originally associated with the mother's feeding her young child. Thus the notion of family that is most important here is one that emphasizes maternal relations, rather than the patriarchal relations of father and son, for the former has strong links between feeding and affection.

PRACTICES REGARDING THE ELITE

The practices of compassionate governing directed toward officials and elite men concern different issues from those aimed at the people. Mencius' proposals regarding elites emphasize the cultural and social importance of taxes, standards, and the ruler's use of men who are wise, virtuous, and capable. A tacit dimension of female gendered behavior continues to be part of the dynamics of the ideas as well, however.

The expansion of Mencian concerns to include the elites is given a historical basis in 3B9. Here, Mencius reviews the past, when the way of the ancient sages declined and chaotic conditions returned. In brief, the Duke of Zhou helped King Wu to restore benevolent government and the practices of the ancient sages. When heretical views and violent behavior appeared once again, Confucius was inspired to compose the *Annals*. Representing heresies, the views of Yang Zhu and Mo Di rejected two of the five relations, ruler and minister and father and son. Without correct thinking, the elites abandoned the five relations and killed their rulers and fathers. According to this passage (from the last textual layer), by the time of Mencius the practices of a true king had expanded from taking care of the people's affairs and feeding the people to restoring correct thinking among the elite. Contributing to this change was the expansion of the sources of chaos from the natural environment, to the people's own lack of order, the barbarians, and finally to the beliefs and behavior of the elite themselves.

As part of his proposed solutions, Mencius recommends that the elites be included in governing (1B7). He advises the ruler not to make important decisions by himself, but to listen to the views of other elites—his close advisers, high officials, and the gentlemen of the state. If the ruler does so in cases of employing those who are lower ranking and virtuous over those of higher rank and not so virtuous, or distant relatives who are virtuous over close ones not so virtuous, or in cases of execution, then, according to Mencius, he will be considered father and mother of the people (*weiminfumu*). In this way Mencius brings the elites into the familial context of governing, although their role is different from that of the children-people. Here those virtuous elites of lower rank become an expansion of the father and mother compassionate ruler, for they also can make decisions and act. They are implicitly like ideal mothers, who are often described by the same term, *xian,* and who are conceived as wise and good but distant in some way from patriarchal power.

Elsewhere Mencius advises the king to honor the virtuous (*zunxian*) and employ those who are capable (*shineng* 使能), so that superior men will be in positions of authority (2A5). If he does so, the elite everywhere will be delighted and will want positions at his court. Here, with the kingly expansion of ruling power, virtue and capability (of lower ranked men) are linked to feelings of delight and approval and to a movement toward, or a return to, the center (of power), the court. As seen in other passages (4A13, 7A22), the idea of returning to the center coupled with good feelings is also implicitly associated with family, returning home, and maternal love.

Mencius further introduces the idea that the ruler must use standards if he is to practice benevolent government (4A1–3). To pacify and rule the empire, it is not enough that the ruler himself be a benevolent person. While his own character is important, he needs to follow a standard, just as artisans and musicians need the compass, square, and pitch pipes. For a true king, the standard is the way of Yao and Shun, the way of the former kings. However, even as he makes the distinction between a ruler's practices and his personal character, Mencius also blurs the distinction. He implies that only a benevolent person (as ruler) would use the benevolent practices of the sages as his standard for ruling, and he must do so if he is to be a benevolent ruler-person.

Standards are abstractions, derived from the particulars of certain experiences and applicable to many different specific situations. The reliance on standards or measuring instruments entails a different emphasis in thinking from that of maternal and farming practices, in which the particulars are a constant concern. In these contexts, absolute standards like those of a compass or a carpenter's square are ultimately unworkable, for the weather varies and children are different. The appeal to a fixed standard reflects a borrowing from the thinking of craftsmen, and in the sphere of government it is a type of thinking often applied to a bureaucracy. While Mencius incorporates the notion that standards are necessary, even for officials and ministers, he relaxes the rigidity of standards by maintaining that standards are a matter of ritual and moral behavior.

The proposed practices of compassionate governing make the Mencian position full of tension and contradiction. In regard to taxes, for instance, Mencius wants to keep taxes at a certain level so as to maintain social distinctions and political order, which are both contrasted to things associated with women, barbarians, a lack of culture, and chaotic conditions. However, in terms of expanding the kinds of men and behavior in the ruling circle, Mencius makes the governing context analogous to the familial context, which has strong associations with mothers and children, with feelings of various kinds—compassion, morality, pleasure, affection, and maternal concern, and with those who are virtuous but without high rank, like (ideal) mothers. Mencius' use of the way of the sages as the standard for governmental practices also implicitly rejects and embraces practices and ideas associated with women, for King Wen is the paramount model. At the same time, of course, through the relations of father and son, husband and wife, and brothers, the family is clearly an institution of patriarchy and its social distinctions. Thus, in promoting patriarchal order and benevolent government, Mencius seems to rely on the fact that men will attend to only some of his ideas while carefully avoiding the implications of others.

Chapter 6

Ruling As Son and Younger Brother

Filiality and Deference of the Ruler

We have seen that the practices of benevolent government require the implementation of economic, political, and educational measures that will improve and bring order to the lives of the people. Although Mencius believes that everyone will benefit from the proposed new practices, he recognizes that people often lack the motivation to change their behavior in significant ways, even to help themselves. Motivation is thus a critical issue, applying to individual persons at all levels of society and to the people as a group. Like many Chinese philosophers, Mencius assumes people need to know what to do before they can do it. He explicitly rejects ruthless behavior, although it can achieve short-term results, since it ultimately destroys more than it achieves. The actions of King Hui of Liang serve as an example of how short term thinking leads to hollow victories, for the king's efforts to extend his territory ultimately led to the demise of even those whom he most loved, his sons and younger brothers (7B1).

In focusing on the moral development of the ruler as a person, especially in terms of the psychological dimensions of his interpersonal relations, Mencius links issues of motivation, learning, knowledge, modeling, and action. He conceives of moral behavior in reference to specific relations and situations within the social-political world, and so self-cultivation entails learning to behave properly, and differently, according to the context. Although the relations of father and son and of ruler and minister are the most important in the text, the relations specifically recognized as the five relations are also mentioned, and they became increasingly important as the Confucian-Mencian tradition developed over time. Whatever the relation is, the participants face certain expectations regarding their feelings and behavior. That is, in addition to the actions to be performed, Mencian interest focuses on personal feelings and their source. Thus the virtues associated with a given relation include specific feelings along with specific types of behavior. Mencius assumes people are motivated both by a genuine understanding of their interests and by their inborn feelings. A further critical assumption is that the ruler's conduct will serve as a model from which others can learn.

In order to become a true king, a benevolent man in the position of authority, the ruler must practice self-cultivation in two contexts, his own family and the state, ideally the empire. He does so by developing himself in the situations that apply to him from among the five relations. In the context of the family, he participates in the relations of father and son and of older brother and younger brother. How the husband-wife relation fits into this schema will be addressed below, but the ruler's efforts to cultivate himself in order to become a benevolent ruler do not include those self-cultivation efforts that help make him a good husband. For the ruler, the critical family relations that he must cultivate to become a benevolent ruler are the two in which a man can behave as either participant in the relation.[1] Cultivating himself in the role of husband does not apply to the ruler here, but it is important for others.[2]

Although these relations consist of a superior and an inferior in terms of sociopolitical status, the person who is the subject, the one seen as initiating responsible action, may be in either the superior or subordinate position. For any particular man, these two relations can therefore expand to six, depending on whether he is the subject or the recipient of action. That is, in the first relation, he must learn the positions of son and of younger brother as the subject, with the aged father and older brother as recipients; in the second relation, he must learn the positions of father and older brother as the subject, with the son and younger brother as recipients; and third, the positions of aged father and aged brother as a recipient, not subject (or initiator), of action. Involved in more than one relation at a time, the ruler would be father in one relation, son in another, and eventually aged parent in another. Although it is important that he behave properly in all his positions, in the context of the family the focus throughout the text is his cultivating the behavior appropriate to the positions of son and younger brother as subjects, or initiators, of responsible action.

The ruler's self-cultivation in the context of the state or empire (as distinct from the family) entails three further and different positions. The first two are the positions of ruler in the ruler and minister relation and friend in the friend and friend relation, while the third is a new position, called father and mother of the people. Like the positions of ruler and friend, this new position functions in the context of the empire, beyond the family, but unlike them, it is not one of the five relations. While it may appear to be similar to the role of father, which occurs inside rather than outside the family, it actually is quite different. This new position is discussed in the next chapter.

Here the concern is the behavioral positions of son and younger brother and the importance of their new meanings in Mencian thought. The position of son is arguably the most critical role, because it functions in both the patriarchal context of the five relations (in the father and son relation) and in the maternal context of mother and son, which is socially important but theoretically outside the patriarchal order, a system of male gendered behavior. The general meanings associated with the son are culturally different in these two contexts, but in Mencian thought they become intertwined. This phenomenon then leads to the concept of father and mother in the context of the empire.

There are several steps that occur. Recognizing that a ruler's ability to govern can be severely hampered by a population that strongly resents the ruler, Mencius proposes a course of action that will help the ruler gain the voluntary cooperation of the people. Evoking the context of parent and child and applying its ideas to that of ruler and ruled, he wants the people to behave like good sons and younger brothers to the ruler, now conceived as a parent-ruler, and also to be good sons, fathers, brothers, and husbands to their own family members. To achieve this transformation in the people's (naturally wild) behavior, the ruler must provide clear models of his several positions (or roles) in his own behavior for how men are to behave.

Mencius teaches that if the ruler is not filial to his own aged parents, other elites will not be filial and loyal to him and the children-people will not be filial either to him or to their own parents. Similarly, if the ruler is not respectful to his aged elders, other elites will not be respectful or deferential to him and the children-people will not be respectful to their superiors and elders. On the other hand, if the king's own behavior is properly filial-benevolent and fraternal-deferential, so will be the behavior of the people, and their newly ritualized behavior will lead to military success and a thriving population.

If the ruler behaves well in his several positions involving family relations, the people will love and support him, as they should a parent, especially a mother. They will take refuge in him. As father and mother in the context of the empire, he will be their home, that is, like a mother to them. What follows next is a symbolic reversal of roles. Instead of being the recipients of the ruler's actions, they (the people) will initiate action, taking the responsibility of treating him (the ruler) like an aged parent by voluntarily following his desires. The ruler thus models moral knowledge, that is, the kinds of behavior that the people and the elite should learn to do, and he models all his relational positions. Particularly important are the shifting perspectives in the positions of son and younger brother.

When the son is the initiator of action and the father the recipient, the son is in the position of responsibility and power, while the father has become the weak and aged one. Among the people, such a son is one of the strong young men (*zhuangzhe*) to which the text often refers. From the perspective of the son, the philosophical focus is on how the adult son treats the aged father, not the reverse. The transformation of the son from the weak and inferior position (that of a young child) to the strong and superior position (as an adult) involves certain ways of behaving that the son learns. Or, at least, Mencius wants him to learn.

Mencian thought uses dynamics of behavior derived from maternal practices to transform the son and younger brother from recipients to initiators of action. In the transformed relationships, both father and son and older brother and younger brother have to learn new kinds of behavior, and in doing so, each side of the relation draws on different aspects of maternal practices. The role of minister or vassal functions for the most part in a comparable way to that of younger brother, except that its sphere is the state rather than the family. In addition, there is no expectation or philosophical consideration, as there is with the father and son relation, that the subject in the ruler and minister relation will eventually change, thereby reversing the position of strength and responsibility.

The fact that some of the most important Mencian moral concepts apply specifically to the positions of son, younger brother, and minister (vassal) indicates their importance. It is not enough for a true king to behave as father and mother of the people; he also must model for the people their reciprocal behavior as sons and younger brothers. The text often pairs these positions, so that the position of son is linked either with younger brother or minister, thus promoting a transcoding of the family and state contexts. For instance, Mencius often speaks of benevolence (*ren*) and rightness (*yi*), and filial piety (*xiao*) and fraternal deference (*ti* 悌) together. The former pair refers to the behavior of son and minister and the latter to the behavior of son and younger brother.

The Complexes of *Ren*, *Xiao*, *Qin*, and *Yi*, *Ti*, *Jing*

Mencian concepts of morality imply particular types of actions, in that they derive from the behavior that constitutes certain specific relations. These concepts are originally not abstractions that could be given content with numerous choices of plausible actions, much as a carpenter's ruler and square can be used to measure various lengths and angles. The specificity of the moral concepts (in terms of both relation and gender) is important, for it is the basis of the dynamics of the Mencian moral-political system. It is critical to the ruler's development into the new kind of ruler, as father and mother of the people, and to later popular support of Confucian-Mencian morality. To support these claims, the following discussion examines the specific kinds of behavior to which Mencius refers with his concepts of morality and his arguments for the necessity of the ruler's modeling moral behavior. The following chapter will then address the concept of father and mother of the people and further evidence for claiming maternal dimensions to Mencian ideas.

As noted previously, the terms *ren* (benevolence) and *yi* (rightness) are paired throughout the text. They are commonly translated and understood as general concepts, but the text suggests that *ren* and *yi* are abstracted from, and in effect summarize, specific actions expected respectively of those in the positions of son and minister.[3] Examination of the text further shows that the three terms, *ren* (benevolence), *xiao* (filial piety), and *qin* (treating your father or parents properly and affectionately, being close to them), form a set of ideas that refer to similar kinds of behavior and entail action by the same subject (the moral adult son) in the relation of father and son. From a functional viewpoint, they have similar meanings. The three terms, *yi* (rightness or dutifulness), *ti* (fraternal deference), and *jing* (respect), function for the most part in a similar way. That is, these three also constitute a set of ideas that refer to similar kinds of behavior and entail the same subject (the moral younger brother or minister) in the relation of older and younger brothers or ruler and minister. Overlapping with both of these sets is another, more general term, *laolao* 老老 (treating the aged properly).

Because of their lack of obvious specificity, the meanings of the more abstract of these terms, benevolence and rightness, often are separated from their contextual source. This abstraction occurs for many reasons, including the reader's exclusion of other passages as a possible part of the context of any particular passage. Although determining the specific context of a passage can be difficult and depends on one's perspective, or the kinds of questions one is asking about the text, it is important to consider the whole text, because its ideas appear in various guises in different passages. Networks of associations provide connections among ideas, even though the actual terms used may differ. Thus, attention should be paid to how ideas function in a context, for different terms can be used for the same particular actions.

Turning to the text, we find that in the opening passage Mencius advises the king to pursue benevolence and rightness and reject personal profit as a course of action (1A1). Near the end of his argument supporting benevolence and rightness, Mencius says, "Not yet has there been a man who is benevolent (*ren*) and yet abandons his father (*qin*). Not yet has there been a man who is dutiful (*yi*) and yet does not defer to (*hou* 後) his ruler." Here Mencius directly links benevolence with filial piety (*xiao*) and dutifulness (rightness) with deference (*hou*, but usually termed *ti*), although the terms *xiao* and *ti* are not literally used. The conversation alludes to the two main spheres of the political context, the patrilineal family and the government. Benevolence and filial piety suggest a man's obligations regarding the former, while dutifulness and deference refer here to a man's duties in governmental service.[4]

Whether benevolence entails other actions is not indicated here, but it means at least a son's behavior of not abandoning his father. Passages elsewhere in the text speak of this behavior in a positive way and sometimes more specific way, as requiring that an adult son take care of his father while he is alive and give him a proper burial after death, that is, not abandon the corpse unburied in a ditch. The second statement, concerning dutifulness (rightness) as a concept paired with benevolence, is comparable. Whether dutifulness entails other actions remains open also, but it means at least that a vassal or minister should defer to his ruler. The minister's relationship to the ruler parallels the son's to the father, the former in the state and the latter in the patrilineal family. Even though they both might have the capability not to do so, the son should not abandon his father and the vassal should yield to his ruler.

The claim that *ren* and *yi* fundamentally mean *xiao* and *ti* respectively is supported by numerous passages. For instance, the comments in 3B4 reveal that *ren* and *yi* are alternate terms for *xiao* and *ti,* and all terms refer to Mencian ideal masculine behavior that the gentlemen embodies. This passage speaks of a man whose behavior is filial inside (at home) and deferential outside (in social-political interactions) and as preserving the way of the former kings. This man is also described as one who practices benevolence and dutifulness and who is a gentleman.[5] In promoting certain actions involved in taking care of one's parents, Mencius combines the expressions filial son (*xiaozi* 孝子) and benevolent man (*renren* 仁人), making them a compound term (in 3A5). This term refers to the filial behavior of properly burying one's parents (*qin*) after their death, as opposed to simply tossing their bodies in the ditches.

In 3B9, referred to briefly in the previous chapter, Mencius claims that in the past at the time of Confucius there were cases of ministers' killing their ruler and sons' killing their father, and now in his own time the views of Yang Zhu and Mo Di are prevalent. With its emphasis on one's personal, selfish interests, Yang's view is equivalent to advocating no ruler, a rejection of dutifulness, while the advocacy of universal love (*jianai* 兼愛), Mo's view, is equivalent to advocating no father, a rejection of filial piety. And further, the denial of ruler and father makes people the same as animals, who are considered to be without social relations, that is, Mencius' ideal kinds of masculine behavior. We should note that the behavior rejected by Mencius, such as pursuit of private profit, is not embodied in any recognized social relation.

The ruler's actions now, in not taking care of the people, are equivalent to the causes of great disorder in the past, namely, flooding, encroaching barbarians and wild animals, and rebellious and murderous ministers and sons. These problems were solved respectively by Yu, the Duke of Zhou, and both the Duke of Zhou and Confucius. Mencius now wants to follow these three sages in their work. Although he claims he is not fond of arguing, he has to contest the views of Yang and Mo, because their ideas lead to unacceptable consequences. Their views and practices block up benevolence and dutifulness.

Yang and Mo symbolize the violation of the two virtues most important to Mencius, namely, filial piety-benevolence (treating father or parents properly, also termed *qin*) and dutifulness-deference (also called respect, *jing*). Mo represents violation of the first virtue and Yang the second. Unlike other passages that focus on the ruler's cultivation of filial piety and deference, or the people's cultivation of the same, here the focus is on men in the ruling elite to cultivate these virtues, expressed here as filiality and dutifulness.

Mencius further says that the fulfillment (or fruit) of the virtues consists of the following: benevolence (*ren*) is serving one's father (*qin*), and rightness (*yi*) is following one's older brothers (recognizing proper order). Wisdom (*zhi* 智) is understanding and practicing these two virtues (*ren* and *yi*), ritual (*li*) is regulating and adorning the practice of these two virtues, and music (*yue* 樂) is delighting in the practice of these two virtues

(4A27). The fullest development of Mencian masculinity thus is serving one's father and following one's older brothers, and practicing this behavior with understanding, with proper regulation, with adornment, and with delight. Moreover, the performance of this behavior is called benevolence and dutifulness. We should emphasize that the subject here is an adult son and younger brother, not a child.[6]

In another passage the terms change to *en* (kindness) and *jing* (respect) in place of *ren* and *yi*, but the importance of the two primary relations is affirmed (2B2). This passage claims that inside the family there is the relation of father and son, while outside the family there is the relation of ruler and minister, and these are the great relations of men. The former relation is based on kindness (*en*) while the latter is based on respect (*jing*). In place of the ruler's cultivating deference and respect within the family, he is here encouraged to develop it outside the family in the empire. Further emphasizing that filial piety and fraternal deference are the foundation for becoming a true king, Mencius claims that all men are capable of becoming a Yao or Shun, the ideal sage kings, and it is a matter of making the effort, not a matter of lacking ability (6B2). Specifically, a man should take these sages as his models of behavior, for the way of Yao and Shun is simply filial piety and fraternal deference.

Mencius makes clear that one's behavior toward others and the concept applied to that behavior depend upon who the other is—a thing, the people, or one's father, and who oneself is in the relationship. What is appropriate in one situation does not apply to all others. In 7A45, for instance, we find some distinctions regarding appropriate behavior that focus on the superficially similar notions of to love (*ai*), be benevolent (*ren*), and to treat properly as a father (*qin*). While not addressing gender per se, this passage does affirm the view that virtues (appropriate ways of behaving) are gendered. A gentleman (*junzi*) loves things (*aiwu* 愛物) but is not benevolent to them. He is benevolent but not affectionate (*qin*) to the people. He treats his father properly with affection (*qinqin* 親親). Here is an example of *qin* meaning *xiao* (filial piety).

Used in some cases with (living) things, love (*ai*) is also used (in 7A15) with the behavior of young children (boys) to their fathers. This passage indicates how the behavior and expected virtues change as the subject changes in his roles. Although benevolence and proper behavior toward one's father are often used as equivalent terms, meaning filial piety, here they are not equivalent. As father and mother of the people, the ruler is benevolent (*ren*) to the people, with a benevolence of maternal kindness and compassion. As son to his father, the same person is filial (*qin*). While *qin* retains the sense of filial piety, *ren* is transformed into a maternal type of kindness that is appropriated by the gentleman who would be a father and mother kind of ruler and is applied here in the political arena, not in the family. Depending on who the subject and recipient are, benevolence can mean filial piety or a maternal-like kindness toward those who are in some respect weaker or inferior. Embodying both senses, the ruler who behaves as a filial son in his family becomes father and mother in the empire.

Implicitly speaking to a (potential) ruler and about moral behavior, Mencius further says that what a man can do without learning is his innately good ability (*liangneng* 良能), and what he can know without pondering is his innately good knowledge (*liangzhi* 良知). All babies and little boys know to love (*ai*) their parents (or, father *qin*); when grown, they all know to respect (*jing*) their older brothers (*xiong*); to treat your father properly and with affection (*qinqin*) is benevolence (*ren*), to respect your elders (*jingzhang* 敬長) is rightness (*yi*). There is nothing else but to extend this kind of behavior to the empire (7A15). In other words, the ruler should model this behavior so that commoner men can also fulfill these moral obligations.[7]

As is evident here, *qin* and *ren* are conceived as filial piety (*xiao*), while *jing* and *yi* are conceived as fraternal deference (*ti*), even though the terms *xiao* and *ti* are not used. The term love (*ai*) is used in connection with children or things, children's love of their parents or a man's love of things (7A45). When the young men grow up and become initiators of action, although still in the socially inferior position to fathers and older brothers, the terms change, to *qin*, *ren*, or *xiao*, and to *jing*, *yi*, or *ti*.

Mencius' view that to govern well the ruler must practice personal cultivation is a way of verbalizing the implicitly metonymic way of thinking. He should be a good son to his father and a good subordinate, like a younger brother, to those socially superior to him. The younger brother shows deference in the family context and beyond it to those who are his elders and superiors, while the minister shows deference in the sphere of government. Since the ruler cannot (simultaneously) be the minister too, rightness (*yi*) for the ruler applies to the family, as does *ren* (benevolence or filiality), but for other men *yi* (dutifulness, rightness) applies to behavior in the three positions of son, younger brother, and minister.

Although the term benevolence is not always explicitly used, the filial behavior to which *ren* (benevolence) refers is thought of as the beginning of the kingly way. Mencius says that the king should make it possible for the people to take care of their parents properly while they are living and mourn them properly after death, so that they will have no regrets (1A3).

And in another passage concerning the king's extension of benevolent government to the people (1A5), we see that the king's own self-cultivation of *ren* and *yi* should result in getting the strong young men to cultivate their filial piety, fraternal deference, loyalty, and good faith, so that within the family they properly serve their fathers and older brothers and in the community they properly serve their elders and superiors.

These virtues apply to men in a specific way, namely, as subjects or initiators of action, while they occupy the politically subordinate position of son and younger brother in the relations of father and son and older and younger brothers. We see here how the sets of associations expand, as the virtues are transcoded across different contexts. That is, the virtues of a man as subject and in the inferior position are *ren* (benevolence) and *xiao* (filiality) toward his father and *ti* (fraternal deference) toward his older brothers. Outside the family and within the context of government and community, the comparable virtues are *yi* (rightness) and *ti* (deference), and *zhong* (loyalty) and *xin* (good faith), toward his elders and superiors. The virtue of deference is located both in the governmental and familial contexts, providing an explicit link in addition to the implicit associations.

Modeling Filial and Deferential Behavior

With the virtues of a minister and younger brother closely associated, Mencius sometimes substitutes younger brother for minister when speaking about dutifulness (*yi*) and deference (*ti*). He does this throughout 4A, where he discusses how to practice the virtues of filial piety (*xiao* or *ren*), on the one hand, and fraternal deference (*ti* or *yi)*, on the other. In 4A4, these virtues are, with some slight modification, mapped onto the four virtues (benevolence, dutifulness (rightness), ritual action, wisdom, *ren*, *yi*, *li*, *zhi*) that constitute the full elaboration of the four beginnings in Mencian thought (discussed below in chapter 8). The shifting viewpoints make this short passage of particular interest, as it addresses the importance of modeling.

Speaking implicitly to the ruler, Mencius says that if the ruler loves others as children (*ai*) but they do not treat him as sons should treat their father (*buqin* 不親), then the ruler should look into how benevolently he treats his own father (*fanqiren* 反其仁). Here Mencius uses the term benevolence (*ren*) in the sense of *xiao* or *qin*. The fact that *qin* is also used in this context indicates Mencius has in mind the specific meaning of filiality for *ren*. The next statement follows the same pattern. Mencius says that if he, the ruler, governs others but they are disorderly, he should look into his own wisdom (*zhi*), that is, his knowing and preferring the proper choices concerning right and wrong behavior. Referring to deference, the third statement follows the same pattern. If the ruler is courteous to others but his courtesy is not reciprocated, he should look into how he respects (*jing*) his own elders. Here Mencius uses the term *jing* (respect) as an alternate term for dutifulness and fraternal deference.

Given that Chinese thinkers widely accepted that people learn from the behavior of others, Mencius stresses the importance of the king's self-cultivation. As the model for behavior, he too should be benevolent-filial within his family and dutiful-deferential beyond the family. He should also learn that the practice of these two types of moral behavior entail specific relations. But the question remains as to how the ruler himself can be dutiful-deferential (*yi*) to a superior if there is no one politically superior to him. The answer lies in processes of association and transformation. As seen in 1A1, *ren* and *yi* apply to two different contexts, respectively the familial and the governmental, but they are also transcoded (as a result of their constant pairing), so that reference to one is also an implicit reference to the other. While all men should practice the same kind of personal cultivation within the family, their political positions require the cultivation of different virtues in the sphere of government. If one has political superiors, one should defer to them. If one does not, as in the case of the ruler, then political deference becomes transformed into fraternal and filial deference, which is behavior in a familial context. The ruler thus becomes associated with others in their positions as sons. The ruler can also model the behavior of a minister by showing respect to a moral advisor (as illustrated in 2B2).

The actual moral behavior of each participant in these relations is critical. Illustrated with the three examples provided above (from 4A4), the message is clear that if the ruler wants others to behave toward him in certain ways, he must exhibit that same behavior in contexts appropriate for him. Since he wants others to behave properly in their inferior positions of sons and younger brothers toward him in the superior position of being like a father or elder brother to them, he must also behave properly as an inferior to those who are superior to him, his father and elders. The success of his performance of his duties as a superior—as father, ruler, and elder, depends on how he performs his duties as an inferior—as son and younger brother. If he does not succeed in his actions as a superior, the answer lies in his inadequate behavior as an inferior.

These ideas about the ruler's modeling the kinds of behavior that he wants the people to embody and about the two complexes of *ren, xiao, qin* and *yi, ti, jing* have relevance to how we interpret the statement of the five relations, mentioned above in chapter 3 (and note 7). A literal interpretation-translation of the statement makes it unclear as to whose behavior is being addressed. However, given the audience of the text, the fact that different positions in a relation require different behavior, and the fact that Mencian thought is attempting to get men to change their behavior in certain ways, a more fitting interpretation would be along the following lines.

There should be affection between father and son: an adult son should treat his elderly father properly, in a filial or benevolent way. This son should take care of his elderly father while he is still alive and should perform the proper rituals upon his death. Although *qin*, in the phrase *fuziyouqin*, has the sense of affection and closeness, it implies the affection of a social inferior (here the adult son) who is morally cultivated toward a superior (here his elderly father). As claimed above, *qin, xiao*, and *ren* form a set of concepts that fundamentally refer to ideal filial behavior. The instruction is how a moral son should behave toward his father, not vice versa. Nothing is said here about the father's behavior, and even if it were as bad as that of Shun's father, the son still should practice this teaching.

There should be dutifulness (rightness) between ruler and minister: a minister should exhibit rightness in his behavior toward his ruler and a ruler should be respectful toward wise advisors. This relation occurs in the context of the state and is parallel to the son's relation to his father in the family. *Yi*, in the phrase *junchenyouyi*, is a general term more abstract than fraternal deference (*ti*) and respectfulness (*jing*), the two concepts with which it is frequently associated. When the emphasis of *yi* is similar to *ti*, this instruction is directed toward the moral minister and the gentleman, who are in the politically inferior positions. However, when *yi* is closer to *jing* in meaning, this instruction can also apply to the ruler, whom Mencius advises to behave respectfully toward a wise, but politically subordinate, teacher or advisor.

There should be separateness between husband and wife: a husband should maintain the proper distinction between his and his wife's duties (*fufuyoubie*). Blurring social boundaries, like agricultural boundaries, is considered detrimental to political order. This relation differs from the others in that it is the only one in this thinking about masculinities that recognizes a place for women, and it is the only relation in which a man cannot occupy both positions. Since the position of mother is not formally in the five relations, this relation of husband and wife keeps women in the system without openly acknowledging the one critical capability women have that men do not, that of giving birth. By stressing differences, this relation helps to deny explicitly the dynamics that implicitly contribute to Mencian thought, namely, the appropriation and transformation of female gendered behavior.

There should be proper order between older (brother) and younger (brother): the younger brother should behave toward his older brothers, literally and figuratively, according to proper order, a duty that in other passages is called fraternal deference and respect (*zhangyouyouxu*). While it is possible that this teaching is directed toward both younger and older brothers, the emphasis in *Mencius* is primarily on the cultivation of virtues appropriate to sons and younger brothers, so that these virtues can be modeled (by the ruler) to the people and to elite men.

There should be trustworthiness between friends (*pengyouyouxin*). As noted previously, Mencius is trying to change the basis of friendship from strategic political alliances to moral behavior, and so we see that the relation of friends occurs between two men, one who is morally cultivated but politically inferior and who may be in the role of teacher, and another who is politically superior and is perhaps but not necessarily a ruler. This instruction is especially, but not exclusively, addressed to the person in the subordinate position. As a political inferior, the (teacher) friend should act with genuineness and good faith toward his superior friend and certainly not attempt to take advantage of his friend's higher position. This relation became extremely important later in the philosophical tradition and was often termed *shiyou* 師友 (teacher and friend).

In sum, Mencian teachings are primarily directed to men as they occupy the subordinate position in a relation, especially that of (adult) son, minister, and (adult) younger brother. As part of establishing a new conception of government, a benevolent government, the ruler must teach and convince those who are stronger to carry out certain social responsibilities to those who are weaker (old and young). The best way to do this is to model the behavior. Thus, using such concepts as *ren*, *xiao*, *qin* and *yi*, *ti*, *jing*, Mencius teaches the ruler and other elite men the moral behavior appropriate to the strong young (adult) men. By cultivating himself the behavior appropriate to sons and younger brothers, the benevolent ruler begins the process of transforming governmental relations into family relations. Moreover, what he learned as a young boy from his mother makes the dynamics of this political transformation fundamentally associated with the dynamics of maternal practices.

Chapter 7

Ruling As Father and Mother of the People

Transformations and New Conceptions

From the Mencian perspective, the ruler's behavior establishes a context according to which actions are interpreted, and his behavior provides the models for how elite and commoner men are to behave. By behaving as if he were father and mother and the people were his children, the ruler establishes the empire as a type of family, one emphasizing maternal practices in addition to patriarchal and patrilineal duties. Parent and child relations become central, taking the place of political relations formerly conceived in terms of a shepherd and his flock of sheep and goats or a strong ruler subduing wild animals and lands. The ruler's behavior as father and mother establishes new ideas both about the relationship between ruler and ruled and of the ruler and ruled themselves. A true or benevolent king must be a good father and mother to the children-people, and they in turn must treat him properly and affectionately as a parent. As previously discussed, to enable the people to achieve the latter, the ruler needs to provide the model of a filial son along with his economic and other measures.

We see the process of transformation by which these new conceptions are formed occurring in the text between the earlier and later layers. Terms having maternal and familial associations are not used to apply to the state in the original interviews or the composite remembered conversations, but they do occur in the added conversations.[1] Father and mother of the people, for instance, is not used for the ruler at first. In the earlier layers the ruler is variously referred to as ruler (*jun* 君), shepherd of men (*renmu* 人牧), king or prince (*wang* 王), and prince (*hou* 侯).[2] None of these terms evokes the maternal or family association that father and mother of the people does.

As this phrase suggests, the developed Mencian position is that the ruler's behavior should resemble that of fathers and mothers. To conceive the ruler like a father turns the sphere of government into one like the family, and by being kind, protective, loving, sympathetic, and compassionate, a fatherly ruler also becomes a motherly ruler. It is safe to say that, if the term father had sufficiently contained these associations by itself, the use of the term mother and the text's references to mothers (especially through association with King Wen) would most likely not have been so necessary. Although the text does not say explicitly that Mencian thought is appropriating maternal behavior in its construction of this new kind of ruler, there are many passages that make the point implicitly.

The new ideas about the ruler and his ruling practices are expressed in several ways, including through the use of particular terms, associations of ideas, indirect references, direct comparisons, and the kinds of behavior advocated. The new terms clearly have emotional associations that especially evoke maternal feelings and practices, since they are used in a familial context or in one modeled after it. As father and mother of the people, the transformed ruler is encouraged to love and protect the people, and to employ and extend kindness. Like a mother, he is called on to be virtuous, and like a wife he is urged to be respectful, thrifty, courteous, and humble (3A3). *Xianmu* 賢母 (wise and virtuous mother) was a standard term for respected mothers throughout most of Chinese history.

As we have seen previously, the ruler's self-cultivation as a filial son occurs in the context of his patrilineal family, and when the people (adult men) learn and practice this type of moral behavior in relation to their own parents, the context is similarly their own patrilineal families. However, when the people practice filial behavior toward the ruler, the context is no longer the family, but the empire. And it is in that governmental context that the ruler becomes father and mother of the people. Not one of the five relations, this new position does not involve a recognized relation within the older conceptions of either the patriarchal family or government. It entails a new form of masculine behavior (by both the ruler and the people). As with other kinds of behavior, the practices of father and mother ruler are part of a relational pair, the other half of which consists of babies or young children. When the parent-ruler is subject (or initiator) of action, the children-people are recipients of action, and the parent-ruler has feelings of concern for them. While Mencius wants young children, or the people, to behave in certain ways, he generally views their behavior as a reaction to the parent's behavior, not as initiated on their own. The concept of young children is different from that of sons, as in the father and son relation, but the people are not just like young children. Like a male who changes relational positions within the family depending on changing contexts and age, the people can do so also.

Before examining further the processes by which the ruler becomes father and mother of the people, we need to consider an issue about consistency in the Mencian position. Specifically, the question is whether the new conception of the ruler as father and mother is consistent with the fundamental Mencian belief in the importance of social distinctions. One reference to the ruler as father and mother of the people occurs in a discussion between Mencius and King Hui of Liang (1A4). Implying what the ruler should do, Mencius tells the king what he should not do, if he truly is father and mother of people. Since the term father is not used by itself here, as it is in the father and son relation, the implication is that characteristics of a mother are important as well as those of a father. Although there thus appears to be a blurring of social positions, those of mother and of father, there actually is not. There is, however, a blurring or expansion of gendered practices, a kind of transgendering—and this kind of blurring of certain boundaries is critical to Mencian thought.

Given the importance of the patriarchal system, the conflation of the practices of certain social roles would be significant—if it were true, because the Mencian system advocates not only the superiority of males over females, but also the strict separation of social functions. In regard to individual persons, the system of the five relations establishes five distinct relationships that have their own appropriate duties, and within the five relations, husbands and wives are to have separate functions. In regard to classes within the empire, the ruling elite, who work with their heart-minds, are distinct from the people, who work with their brawn (3A3, 3A4). Among the people the occupations are clearly separated theoretically, with farmers, artisans, and merchants as the three recognized categories of the people's occupations. Moreover, in regard to gender, these occupations are male, not both male and female. In addition to advocating clear distinctions in social roles, gender, and class, Mencius explicitly rejects any blurring of these distinctions. As discussed above, Mencius opposes the agricultural position of Shen Nong, the Divine Farmer, because it blurs a class, occupation, and work line between ruler and farmer and distinctions based on gender (3A4), and he claims one of the functions of taxes is to maintain political distinctions deemed necessary for civilization (6B10).

Other types of people, work, and practices certainly existed in actuality, but these other types of masculinities were not seen as critical to the political discourse among philosophers. These other types did not have political functions that linked them to the five relations and the four recognized occupations. Since Mencian philosophical thought only addresses male behavior, the activities of mothers could be subsumed under those of the father, thereby ensuring that maternal behavior could remain an implicit and unrecognized part of the social order. It is thus significant that the specific type of female who appears in the new, kingly ruling context, which seems to obscure distinctions in gendered practices, is the mother. Since the position of mother has no theoretical place in a system of male behavior, there is no blurring of social role distinctions. The Mencian advocacy of gender, class, and other kinds of distinctions is not violated or challenged by viewing the ruler as father and mother of the people because only those in the system are relevant. Although important, the mother and child relation is considered a natural relation, as opposed to a social relation, and the philosophical disputes over masculinities involve social relations.

What distinguishes maternal practices from other female gendered practices (such as weaving) is that the practices of a mother are concerned with giving birth to and raising her (or someone's) children. They (the practices) are assumed to be natural, not socially learned initially. Although it may be the same person, what she does as wife in taking care of her husband and his parents, differs from what she does as mother in giving birth and raising the children, supposedly with love, kindness, and protectiveness. By merging the mother's female gendered practices with those male gendered practices of the father in the context of the empire, but not the family, Mencius incorporates the theoretically unacknowledged practices of mothers into the authority position and practices of the father and ruler. Maternal behavior is made an essential part of the Mencian philosophical system by the father's appropriation of the characteristics of the mother's practices. At the same time, Mencian teachings about maintaining distinctions apply to recognized social roles and activities, not to practices outside the system, and so are maintained without conflicts.

Although women offer various kinds of challenges to patriarchal authority, wives are important to the social order, and a wife's duties to serve her husband link her behavior to a son's filial duties to his parents. For instance, a mother instructs her daughter who is about to be married that she must be respectful, cautious, and obedient to her husband (3B2). The text further comments that the way of concubines and wives recognizes compliance as what is right. We also learn that a man takes a wife at least in part to take care of or nourish (*yang*) his parents, thus incorporating her expected behavior into his. Mencius compares the situation of a gentlemen's having to take office because of poverty with that of taking a wife for the purpose of having her take care of his parents (5B5). A man should not do either one, but there are times when he must do such things. Note that, of the various situations Mencius could have chosen for comparing the impoverished gentleman's dilemma, he chooses a situation not in the governmental sphere, but in the family and concerning women. Although the explicit message here concerns grounds for taking office, this passage provides a link to women's practices through the indirect acknowledgment that a wife's duty is to take care of her husband's parents.

Appropriating Maternal Behavior

The question now is how the ruler transforms himself from son (in the father and son relation) within the family to father and mother (of the people) within the empire. As discussed above, the ruler's behavior provides the model for how elite (and commoner) men are to behave, and he wants them to behave as good sons toward him conceived as a parent. If the ruler himself is not filial to his aged parents, neither will others be filial to him, even though he loves them as parents love their children. If the ruler is not respectful himself to his elders, neither will others be respectful to him, even though he is courteous to them. However, if the ruler himself behaves correctly in his own inferior roles, the people will support him and he will be successful in ruling them with a benevolent government. He will be their home, like a mother to them, because like a mother he (ideally) takes care of and has compassion for the weak. The ruler transforms his behavior as son and younger brother into that of father and mother of the people by enabling the people to treat him as such.

My claim of a maternal dimension to Mencian concepts of male behavior rests to a great extent on the incorporation into ideal male behavior of certain activities believed to be particularly or exclusively characteristic of mothers and their practices. Such activities include giving birth, feeding, taking care of and teaching the very young, exhibiting feelings of compassion, caring, and putting the concerns of others before one's own. The discussion in the remaining section of this chapter and in the next chapter will focus on textual support for this position and address the topic of the heart and inborn feelings.

The maternal dimensions of Mencius' thinking are apparent in various ways and in many passages. In 4A4, for instance, Mencius includes an indirect reference to the maternal context by claiming that when the ruler behaves correctly, the empire will take refuge (*gui*) in him. As noted previously, the notion of taking refuge, or returning, is culturally associated with mothers and home. The link to maternal associations is further established here with a concluding quote from the *Odes* that refers to King Wen, whose virtue is associated with that of his mother (Mao 235). Behaving in ways that recall certain maternal practices indicates the process by which the ruler becomes more than just a ruler.

The above instruction for the ruler is repeated in 4A12 with the addition of the centrality of feelings of trust and pleasure. That is, if you want (inferior) others to respond in certain ways to you as a superior, you must be a good model yourself when in an inferior position. If the ruler (as superior) is to gain the (hearts of the) people and so rule them successfully, he must gain the confidence of his own superior when he is in an inferior position. To gain his superior's confidence, he must be trusted by his friends when he is in an inferior position. To gain the trust of his friends, he must serve and please his father.

By following the social norms of relations and so demonstrating his moral cultivation in the position of inferior, he can be successful in the superior position of ruling the people. In part, this is due to his serving as a model and teacher, but it also is due to the Mencian belief that moral power is stronger than military power. The strength of moral power derives in great part from its basis in the heart and its feelings, which are linked to maternal power and the refuge that a good mother provides through her supposedly natural feelings of compassion and love. The goal is to transform the mother's supposedly unconditional love for her child into the people's unconditional love for their parent-ruler. This process is mediated through the son who ideally learns this love from his mother, and then in a reciprocal way he practices this behavior of love toward her (and his father). When he becomes ruler, he exhibits this behavior of love toward the people as his mother did to him, and the people respond by in turn loving him.

Illustrating this process while symbolically transforming the mother into the father, Mencius claims that one cannot become a (fully cultivated) man if one does not please one's father (*qin*), and one cannot become a (fully cultivated) son if one does not follow one's father (4A28).[3] The text goes on to say that once Shun was able to please his father, that is, become a filial son, the empire was transformed and the way was set for all men to behave properly in the relation of father and son. Although their family contexts are different, both King Wen and Shun serve as models of men who become good rulers by behaving as filial sons. King Wen patterns his virtuous behavior on his mother's, whereas Shun becomes filial while overcoming an evil stepmother.

A further dimension of moral behavior is that it developed from and was seen in terms of ritual. Mencius helps to expand ritual-moral concepts of the duty of serving (*shi*) by applying them to a broader range of people than elites previously did and by tacitly incorporating in them aspects of maternal behavior, such as feelings of caring and compassion. This expanded sense of serving is indicated especially by the use of the term *yang* (nourishing, feeding, taking care of), and it has historical precedents particularly in the *Odes*. When explicitly mentioning the father and older brothers, Mencius does not use the term *yang* (nourish) but only uses *shi* (serve). If the terms father and mother are used explicitly, a man may either *yang* (nourish) or *shi* (serve) them. The differences suggested by nourishing and serving reflect the changes in behavior that Mencius is advocating. Mencius comments, for instance, that mourning a father is certainly the time for exerting oneself fully (3A2).[4] The text then proceeds to quote Zengzi: "Serving him according to ritual when he is alive and burying him and giving him sacrifices according to ritual when he is dead—this may be called filial."[5] Given the close association between King Wen and his mother, it is significant that elsewhere King Wen is said to have nourished (*yang*) the elderly (4A13).

The two textual passages regarding Mencius' burial of his mother, a ritual-moral-filial duty, reveal this emphasis in Mencian thought. In the later of the two passages (2B7), Mencius' defense of providing his mother with a more elaborate burial than his father includes a strong appeal to his feelings (*renxin* 人心, human heart) as well as to ritual requirements. The original defense (in 1B16), offered on Mencius' behalf, only relies on his improved financial circumstances.

In addition to proper burial, filial and fraternal duties explicitly include providing for the feeding and clothing of one's father and mother, just as a mother would her young child. According to 1A3, the young men are to be taught filial and fraternal duties, so that they (when grown men) will take care of their elders—that is, not abandon them to struggle on their own to survive. In 1A5, the text claims that bad rulers interfere with the people's livelihood so much that they (the adult men) are unable to nourish (*yang*) their fathers and mothers. As a result, their fathers and mothers are cold and hungry, and their older and younger brothers, wives, and children become separated from each other.

Several passages about Shun reveal the difficulty that a filial son has in fulfilling his duties when his parents are not moral themselves. In one passage about Shun, we see some important assumptions about the responsibilities of a good son and a good father and mother, as well as the way in which the maternal dimension implicitly functions in Mencian thinking (5A1). Even though Shun was a model of filial piety, his father and mother did not love (*ai*) him and he was unable to please them. A good father and mother should love their son, however, and the fact that his did not love him made him extremely distressed. A good son should please his parents, too, not just take care of their needs, but Shun's inability to do so made him feel as if he were a homeless man. That is, there was no one for him to take refuge in and no place in which he felt at home. Although home and love are fundamentally associated with women and the mother's inside, domestic sphere, the father also takes on this association. This transfer is possible because the father represents the family, and with the mother not theoretically present in the system, her characteristics, especially the natural feelings of love that a mother is assumed to have toward her children, merge into his.

Also in this passage, as in other passages, women other than mothers are recipients of action and are lumped together with other recipients or objects. Mothers, however, are different. This passage lists things that all men supposedly want, but none are sufficient to lessen Shun's anxiety from not being loved by and not being able to please his parents. Mencius claims that men want to please the gentlemen of the empire or ruling elites; they want beautiful women, wealth, and high rank; and they want to please their parents. Note that men want (as objects) high rank, wealth, and beautiful women, but they want to please elite gentlemen and their parents. In contrast to the latter desire, the former desire does not involve an interactive relationship. Also listed here are the successive things that a man normally desires over the course of his life. When young, he desires his parents. After learning about women, he desires those who are young and beautiful. After marriage, his desires are directed toward his wife and children. Once he obtains an official position, his desires focus on his ruler and on his ruler's view of him. Only a great filial son like Shun, however, focuses on his parents all his life.

The message here is that people expect a man to shift his desires over his lifetime, but great filial piety demands that a man be extraordinarily attentive to his parents throughout his life. A conflict between loyalty to one's parents and to one's wife, children, and ruler is suggested. Through the use of a term of feeling (*mu* 慕, desire, love, long for) and by the inclusion of the mother, this passage implies that this conflict is fundamentally maintained by its link to mothers. A man could simply do his duty to his father, and not long for his father and mother, but just as his mother loves her son all her life, so he also loves her. Since Mencius does not discuss in a theoretical way the issue of love for one's mother as part of a man's ritual duties, yearning simply for his mother would not have an important place in this (patriarchal) ritual-moral code. His yearning must be for both mother and father. Great filial piety thus is not the ordinary type of filial piety involving the father and son relation but is a special concept that enables relations between mother and son to be acknowledged.

The resulting conflict of loyalty suggests that challenges to patriarchal behavior are associated more with women as wives than with women as mothers. In 3B10, for instance, we find that Mencius is critical of a man who does not live up to his patriarchal duty of keeping the family intact. Although Chen Zhongzi is considered to be a sincere and pure gentleman by Kuang Zhang, Mencius criticizes Chen Zhongzi for doing certain things that make him an unfilial son, so much so that Mencius compares Chen's way of life to that of an earthworm. Chen Zhongzi earns a living by weaving (or making) sandals, and his wife contributes by twisting threads of hemp. That is, she does the spinning and he does the weaving, and they trade their products for the necessities of life. Although Chen Zhongzi comes from an established family, he refuses to live in his older brother's house or eat his food, because he considers his brother's income and house to be gained by immoral means. Thus Chen Zhongzi lives with wife, away from his older brother and mother, although still in the same village. He does visit them, but on one visit he vomited up the goose his mother had cooked after he learned it was the goose that he had previously seen in the yard. Mencius criticizes Chen Zhongzi because he will not eat his mother's food or live in his brother's house and instead eats his wife's food and lives with her in the same village.

The fact that Mencius regards this behavior as extreme and not even human, but like that of an earthworm, clearly suggests the central importance of the two virtues filial piety (applied to the mother here, with the assumption that the father is not alive) and fraternal deference. To live in the same village but not eat his mother's food and not live in his older brother's house violates these virtues, for the latter actions represent keeping the family together. By not doing these things and by doing women's (a wife's) work of weaving, Chen Zhongzi further represents a challenge to the Confucian-Mencian view about social distinctions.

While it is assumed that mother and son have an inseparable relationship (because it is a natural relationship), the same is not so for father and son. Thus Mencius stresses the importance of keeping intact the family—father, sons, and brothers. The separation of father and son as a result of economic hardship is considered even worse than starving to death (7B27). This passage claims that a benevolent ruler emphasizes only one type of tax at a time, because if he emphasizes two, some among the people will starve to death, and if he employs all three (taxation in the form of cloth, grain, and labor), then father and son will separate. Separation of father and son means the destruction of the (patrilineal) family, and so it is worse than starvation, for the father-son relationship is critical to maintaining social-political order. Thus, the duty to keep the family (father and son) together is paramount.

Another passage that affirms the value of keeping the patrilineal family intact is 4A18, which also presents the idea of how to gain moral authority, as opposed to the social-political power one would have from being in a superior position in one of the five relations. In speaking about the relationship between father and son, Mencius says that a gentleman should not teach his own son. The argument is that teaching involves correction (*zheng* 正), which is a matter of demanding goodness (*zeshan* 責善). If the son does not subsequently behave correctly, the father will become angry. The two will then hurt each other and, as the son charges the father with not providing a model of what he is teaching, they will become estranged. And estrangement is the greatest misfortune of all. Thus this passage not only reinforces the notion that exhibiting moral behavior oneself is necessary for having any moral authority over others, it also affirms the duty of keeping the patrilineal family intact.

A polarity is established here between relations and behavior within the family and those outside the family. Goodness is applied to the proper behavior in relationships outside the family, and the notion of correction here reinforces the idea that norms and standards are involved, as distinct from feelings of affection and kindness. This passage does not mention the appropriate behavior of the father to son, or son to father, within the family, but it does say that estrangement must be avoided.

The message in 4B30 sets up even more clearly the difference between appropriate behavior within the family between father and son and in society between friends. In presenting his concept of the benevolent king, who must be a good son in the family in order to be a good father and mother in the empire, Mencius both wants to maintain the patriarchal distinctions of the five relations and create a new position that is shaped by the behavior of mother. By reading 4A18 and 4B30 together, we see that the notion of correction (*zheng*) related to teaching is conceived as demanding goodness (*zeshan*). The idea of goodness entails standards, norms, and rules of appropriate behavior and applies outside the family. As the text in 4B30 says, demanding goodness is the way of friends. If such behavior is applied to the father and son relation, it steals the kindness (*en*) between them. What Kuang Zhang did was to have a disagreement with his father about goodness and so was not allowed near him. As a result, Kuang Zhang sent his own wife and sons away, even though he did not want to, because to remain with them but not with his father challenged social-moral order. It was unfilial. Women, here as wives, are thus associated with practices that are harmful to the Mencian view of social order.

Further comments in 4B30 about unfilial behavior illustrate through negative example appropriate behavior by the son in the father and son relationship. If a king is to rule the people successfully by becoming father and mother of the people, he must avoid the kinds of unfilial behavior mentioned here. Thus, he should see to it that his aged parents are properly nourished, are not shamed, and are not endangered as a result of his own moral looseness. Unfilial behavior is described as, first, not taking care of the nourishment of one's father and mother because of laziness, because of gambling and drinking, because of too much love of one's own property and wealth, and because of partiality toward one's own wife and sons; second, bringing shame to one's father and mother by indulging in sexual desires; and third, endangering one's father and mother by quarrelsome and aggressive behavior. Note that whereas the father and mother are the recipients of the son's filial behavior, his wife is treated as an object similar to his excessive attention to money matters. In addition, his indulgence in sexual desires, which involve women, is what brings shame to his parents, not his laziness, gambling, drinking, excessive attention to money matters, favoring his wife, or aggressiveness. Thus, mothers are the only females deserving deferential treatment, while wives and entertainment women are treated as possible threats to the social order.

Here, Kuang Zhang treated his father as a friend by demanding goodness of him, and this behavior, not the five kinds of bad behavior noted above, made Kuang Zhang estranged from his father. Although Mencius did not agree, others regarded this violation of norms to be just as immoral as the above examples of unfilial behavior, in that they all undermined the five relations. The text indicates that Kuang Zhang wanted the relationships of husband and wife (*fuqi*) and of sons and their mother (*zimu*), but as self-punishment for his unfilial behavior, he sent his wife and sons away, and he would not let his wife and sons take care of (*yang*) him. Thus there is the recognition here that the wife's duty is to nourish or take care of her husband, and that the relationship of son and mother is important.

Since Kuang Zhang did properly take care of his parents, did not shame them, and did not endanger them, Mencius disagrees with the others' judgment of his behavior. Mencius' concern is the disintegration of the father and son relation and the resulting separation of the family, due to the son's wrong behavior. The son's reprimand of the father meant that the son was not exhibiting kindness or filiality to his father. By sending away his own son, Kuang Zhang was allowing the family to separate. From this example, we see that Mencius recognizes the possible tension between a man's duties to his father and his duties to his wife and children.

In the contrast between the adult son's kindness to his father (which may be seen as a transformation of his mother's kindness to him as a young child) and the encouragement of goodness (*shan*) between friends, we see an opposition between "inner" or family and "outer" or society. Kindness from the son refers to filial piety with an acknowledgment of its inclusion of a dimension of feelings. Kindness is not a subset of goodness, for demanding goodness in a relationship that requires kindness will destroy the relationship and its feelings. Implicitly set up here is a contrast between two sets of associations: kindness, son, feelings, the heart, mother, family, inner; and goodness, norms, thinking, friends, society, outer. Morality as goodness is outer and of society, while kindness and love are inner and of family, home, mother-transformed-into-son. This case thus indicates how Mencius transforms the maternal son in the family to the maternal father and mother of the people in the empire.

Shun's filiality also ties in here. Mencius says that Shun married without telling his father in order to avoid the most unfilial behavior of all, not having an heir (4A26). Carrying on one's lineage is a male equivalent of a woman's giving birth. If there is no heir, the family cannot be kept together and cannot be reborn every generation. An indirect reference to the maternal dimension appears at the end of 6B2, in which Mencius claims that the way (of Yao and Shun, or of filial piety and fraternal deference) is like a broad road. If one returns home and looks for it, one will find plenty of teachers. As noted previously, home is the domain especially of the mother and women, and a man practices filial and fraternal duties in reference to the home, toward his parents and older brothers. Even though the son and younger brother are socially in the inferior position, as moral adults they are the responsible subjects, and so their practices have a fundamental pattern of the (morally) strong taking care of the (young or old) weak with love and compassion, which is the pattern of the mother-child relation.

This pattern is the foundation of Mencius' view of social-political order. In 6B4, for instance, Mencius attempts to persuade Song Keng not to argue against war on the basis that it is not profitable, for profit would then become the motive for soldiers to retire from the army, and for how a minister would serve his ruler, how a son would serve his father, and how a younger brother would serve his older brother. The pattern of these relations is the same in that they concern how a man in an inferior position serves his superior. If profit, rather than benevolence and dutifulness, is the motive, the ruler will eventually perish. But if minister, son, and younger brother all embrace or cherish (*huai*) benevolence and dutifulness in serving ruler, father, and older brother, the ruler will become a true king.

This passage clearly indicates that benevolence and dutifulness are virtues that apply specifically to the relations of father and son, older brother and younger brother, and ruler and minister by analogy, and specifically in the sense of the latter's behavior to the former. Even if the desire for profit is based on inborn feelings of desire, just as benevolence and dutifulness are based on inborn feelings of compassion and shame, profit must be rejected as a motive because it does not lead to moral power. The Mencian social order requires that the morally (and, where possible, politically) strong look after those who are weaker. An adult son must take care of his aged father, and adult inferiors must do the same with aged superiors. If relationships are simply a matter of profit, men will survive only as long as they are strong. Aged fathers and superiors will be over-powered, and perhaps left to die, once they become older and weaker. Thus, in these relationships, Mencius must eliminate motives for behavior other than the virtues of benevolence and dutifulness, which he claims are ultimately derived from inborn feelings and from *tian* and which enable the political inferior to be in the subject position of responsibility as a result of cultivating morality.

Although there is no explicit mention of the mother and child relationship here, the use of the term *huai*, to cherish or embrace, evokes ideas of maternal love and feeding and so also her natural feelings of love and compassion. By using the term *huai*, rather than some other term without affective connotations, Mencius makes an implicit link between the virtues of benevolence and dutifulness, or a son's filial behavior toward his father, and the mother's compassionate behavior toward her child.

The strength that one derives from behaving morally while in a socially or politically inferior position is an important part of the developmental process enabling one to become a true king. It resembles the behavior of women who are mothers and yet occupy the subordinate position of wife. Establishing an implicit association with morally powerful mothers who are also politically inferior wives, Mencius presents an account of great leaders who supposedly rose from humble backgrounds (6B15): Shun from the fields, Fu Yue from the builders, Jiao Ge from fish and salt merchants, Guan Yiwu (Zhong) from prison officials, Sun Shuao from the sea (while hiding), and Baili Xi from merchants of the market. Although the usual interpretation is that Shun was a commoner, it is likely that Shun was in the fields to escape his evil stepmother who was trying to kill him, and so adversity is personified as Shun's evil stepmother. The claim is that, before *tian* (conditions) conferred great burdens on these men, it tested and toughened them, making them suffer in various ways. Mencius further claims that the survival of a state depends not only on lawful families and reliable gentlemen inside, but also on threats of enemy invasions from outside. The final claim is that one survives in adversity but dies in ease and comfort. This is a powerful teaching for one who is in a politically weak but morally strong position, as is a mother, a political inferior, or a true king ruling over a small state. It provides immense motivation to endure and understand any kind of suffering for the sake of achieving great things.

In 7A18, we find a similar message concerning adversity and motivation. This passage claims that it is through adversity that men attain virtue and wisdom. Because he is cautious and careful, an orphaned minister or a son of a concubine succeeds when most others fail. This message is implicitly associated with mothers by the singling out of two types of men that are especially linked to mothers, the son of a concubine and an orphan. Here the term orphan is used metaphorically, so that the reference is to a minister who is estranged from or who has lost his ruler. The term orphan is applied to a son without a father, even though he has a mother. In both situations the mother is the active parent and the father or father-ruler is distant by death or by choice. Thus it is her teaching that her son learns, namely, that enduring adversity and suffering can motivate one to succeed in great matters.

The blending of contexts and the transformation of behavior to create the new concept of mother and father of the people is seen in many other forms. In 5A4, aged and in a weaker position, the father is the recipient of his son's moral actions. Referring to Shun and his father, Mencius states that the greatest thing a filial son can do is to honor his father. And the greatest thing he can do in honoring his father is to nourish (*yang*) him with the empire, thus becoming like a father and mother to his father. The transformation of the ruler is also found indirectly in 7A45, where *ren* is transformed from the virtue of benevolence-filiality to one's parents, to benevolence-kindness and protection (such as *bao*) to the people. When he is a child, a man's parents are the source of his being, and when he becomes a kingly ruler, the people are the source of his being. That is, a benevolent ruler gains his authority to rule, or is politically born, from the people, and specifically their hearts or feelings.[6]

In developing the concept of the benevolent king, the text both blurs the distinction between state and family and keeps them separate. By emphasizing the transgendering of behavior, from what is maternal, wifely, and female to the ruler who is conceived as father and mother of the people, Mencius makes gender centrally involved in his new conception of the ruler and his practices of self-cultivation and ruling. To reiterate, the king, in the context of the empire, takes on the moral characteristics of mother and wife in the family by means of an inversion in his familial relations, in which he is the son and younger brother. As son and younger brother, the man who is king is filial-benevolent to his father (or parents), while in ruling the people, he becomes compassionate-benevolent like his mother toward him. As father and mother ruler, he turns the people into his children, who should be filial and benevolent to him.

Although politically inferior to the ruler, the people can become morally superior if the ruler does not cultivate himself. Moreover, the moral superior is the one with ultimate authority, not merely to rule, but to give birth and promote life. The transformations and appropriations do not stop here, but continue in other variations that include, for instance, the mother and *tian*. If the ruler is successful as father and mother of the people, Mencius asserts that the ruler will have no opposition in the empire and will be an officer of *tian*, implying that *tian* is the source of political authority and of the "right" to rule (2A5). Given the associations of *tian* with birth and the source of things, which are associated with mothers, this statement implicitly links the ruler who is a true king with maternal practices. The true king gives birth to the people by becoming father and mother of the people. And, the people become good sons and younger brothers only with a father and mother ruler.

Maternal Associations in Conversations

A further look at a few of the conversations will help demonstrate how the processes of appropriation worked to effect a transformation in the conceptions of the ruler and the people, from master over what is wild and other to parent taking care of children.

In 1A6 (original interview), water is an important symbol. In the form of timely rains, it is used as a symbol for a kingly ruler and in the form of rushing downward as a symbol of the people's unstoppable support of a kingly ruler. Young rice plants are a symbol for the people, who are nurtured by the timely rains of the ruler's paternal actions. Just as young rice plants will dry up and not grow without timely rains, so the people will suffer if the ruler pursues a policy of killing, rather than kindness. However, they will take refuge in him as surely as flooding water flows downward if he stops destructive policies.

Water is associated with the source of life, fertility, young growth, and so also with females as mothers. Claiming that the empire can only be settled by unity and unity can be achieved only by a ruler who does not love to kill others, Mencius compares such a ruler with timely rains and claims that the people will take refuge in him like water's rushing downward. Although shepherd of men is the term used for the ruler here, a term without maternal associations, other terms do have such associations. In addition to water, taking refuge in (or returning) has strong maternal associations, with its allusion to home, the center of life, marriage, and so also to mothers. This passage thus draws on the maternal-related symbolic cluster that includes water, fertility, plants, birth, growth, the one, marriage, and returning home, and it transfers these ideas to the true king and his benevolent rule.

In 1A7, Mencius instructs the king on using kindness (*en*). He advises the ruler to treat the aged in his own family with proper respect (*laowulao*) and extend this treatment to others' aged (*renzhilao* 人之老). "*Laowulao*" combines both filial and fraternal behavior (*xiao* and *ti*, as well as "*qinqin*" and "*jingzhang*," which appear in 7A15). Old and young are paired together, so that Mencius continues with the advice to treat the young properly, in the ruler's own and in others' families. Here, the young (*you*) refer to very small children, not to younger brothers, who are either adults or are older boys. By urging the ruler to take care of the elderly, Mencius is instructing him to behave like a son, younger brother, and wife, all subordinate positions. Since taking care of the young is a maternal activity, Mencius is also urging the ruler to behave like a mother. In this case, the ruler behaves like one who is both in the socially inferior position as son and younger brother and in the subject position as a result of his moral behavior, with his father and older brothers as the recipients of his actions.

In other words, despite his position of political superiority and power, the ruler is urged to behave in two new ways—first like a subordinate in the position of a son, younger brother, and wife toward the aged, and second, like one who is a moral superior as a good mother, as a father and mother, or a motherly kind of father to the young. The first is a patriarchal role; the second is outside the theoretical patriarchal order. By coupling kind and proper treatment of the aged with similar treatment of the young, Mencius establishes a maternal association that is linked to all of the ruler's roles. Typically reserved for the young and weak, maternal kindness is explicitly applied in *Mencius* to the old and weak. The son should behave toward his parents as a mother behaves toward her infant. Even further, the son learns this behavior from his mother's treatment of him. With his mother as a model, he knows how to put himself in a mother-like position and so practice compassionate behavior (which is also wife-like behavior) toward his elderly parents, who are now in the child position.

The maternal connection is indicated in several ways and includes the duties of both a mother and a wife. The ruler in effect should behave toward the aged as someone does who is both a wife and mother. Along with treating the aged properly (her husband's parents) as wife, treating the young properly was part of the mother's work, and here it is also assumed by the ruler. As the ruler behaves in this way, he becomes the father and mother of the people. Mencius says that the ruler should take this heart, that is, his feelings of compassion, that he applies within his family and apply it to others in the empire. Just like a mother with her baby, if he extends his kindness (*tuien*), his actions will be sufficient to protect (*bao*) all within the four seas. If he does not, he cannot even protect his wife and children (1A7). He cannot even do what his wife as mother would do in protecting her children.

Slightly later in this same passage, we see further how farming, mothers, and the heart are associated with each other. Mencius claims that only a gentleman is able to have constant moral feelings (constant heart *hengxin*) without constant work (*hengchan*). The people, however, will not retain constant moral feelings and will behave immorally without constant work. Having a constant heart conveys the idea of having and practicing constant moral feelings, the most fundamental of which are those feelings of compassion and kindness for the old and young that (supposedly) characterize a mother-wife. Thus, the constant production of crops by the people (farmers) is implicitly associated with the constant production of the shoots or beginnings of morality that are in the heart, particularly a mother's heart.

Here we see how the Mencian position includes two separate perspectives and messages. Speaking from a perspective that is superior and strong in moral terms but is inferior and weak in social-political terms, as Mencius' own position was vis-à-vis the ruler, the text stresses that the superiors and the strong should take care of the inferiors and the weak. Taking the viewpoint of the superior and strong, however, his teachings stress obedience by the inferior and weak. The moral strength of the ruler will (supposedly) lead to political strength, and the moral strength of one in a superior position politically is demonstrated by how one voluntarily takes care of the weak, whether the weak are in a superior or subordinate position in social-political terms in other contexts. Although the inferior and the weak should obey regardless of the ruler's moral strength, Mencius knows that such obedience is harder to obtain in the case of cruel rulers. The strategy for the benevolent ruler, the father and mother of the people, thus involves a type of inversion, in that he employs for himself the strategy of one who is inferior and weak in social-political terms. Since an inferior is politically weak, he can be powerful only so far as he can establish himself in the moral position. Thus an inferior must behave morally as a way to establish some superiority. So here, too, in behaving as a good son and younger brother (and mother-wife), the ruler follows this approach.

In 1B7 Mencius presents a further view on how the ruler should behave to be truly the father and mother of the people. In the cases of whether to promote a virtuous man over others with higher rank, or remove someone from office, or put a man to death, the ruler should not just listen to his close advisors and the high officials. He should investigate and act only after listening to the gentlemen of the state. As noted previously, Mencius wants the ruler to behave so that the elites and the people submit to his rule voluntarily, and he assumes that this can only be done with kindness, not with force and cruelty (2A3–5). By allowing those not in the highest positions to contribute to decisions, the ruler would be behaving in a way similar to a mother's kindness toward her vulnerable and weak, but potentially rebellious, child. Although force could be employed, kindness supposedly gains a type of cooperation that does not also entail covert rebelliousness and so is different from that gained by force. The ruler who is father and mother of the people employs a mother's type of kindness along with a father's type of authority.

Referring to a saying from Qi that uses the ideas of timeliness and tools, Mencius further links maternal and agricultural ideas to kingly rule (2A1). The saying maintains that it is better to take advantage of the right opportunity than to start just because you have the knowledge, and it is better to wait for the right season than to start simply because you have a hoe. Doing things according to the right time or circumstances is recognized as a more critical aspect of success than knowledge or tools. In a similar vein and speaking of the overflowing *qi* 氣, Mencius compares its birth and growth to young rice shoots (2A2). You have to nourish them constantly but you cannot forcibly pull at them (like the man from Song) or ignore them (like those who do not weed). The growth (here, of benevolent feelings and practices) has to come from a source within and in a timely way, in the cases of plants, children, and moral behavior.

Five ways by which a gentleman teaches all have implicit associations with maternal and farming practices (7A40). These methods consist of transforming (*hua* 化) like timely rain, helping to fulfill virtue (*chengde* 成德), helping to develop talent (*dacai* 達財), answering questions (*dawen* 答問), and setting an example through personal virtuous (female-like) behavior (*sishuyi* 私淑艾). The processes of transforming, fulfilling, developing, and responding are all interrelated and closely associated with those of birth and growth found in the farming and maternal contexts, while the final method brings in the importance of models and is implicitly associated with female virtue. The use of these two contexts as the relevant analogies indicates that the concern is with processes of growth, which suggest a different idea from meeting a fixed standard, as the artisan analogies suggest.

Mencius thus says that a craftsman can give the standards to another, but he cannot make someone else skillful in their use (7B5). The other's becoming skillful is akin to what a mother is attempting to accomplish in teaching her child, or a gentleman his student. Answering questions indicates that growth is in part due to one's interactions with surrounding contexts. In effect, students, children, and even plants contribute to their growth by initiating events in some way. Teaching through personal example has been discussed previously, with the view proposed that the son's filial behavior (to his father or parents) is implicitly patterned after the mother's kind and loving behavior toward him, her child. The ruler can only become father and mother of the people if he is a filial son. If filial, the people themselves continue the same pattern of behavior toward their parents and the ruler. This maternal and political dynamic continues with each new generation. Behavior originally from the maternal and elite family context is transformed into the context of the state and empire, and then the state becomes a political family, consisting of the (father and mother) ruler and the (children) people.

As discussed previously, the conception of the people changes along with the transformation of the ruler to father and mother. The significance is that rather than simply obeying, the people become children-people and so must learn to treat their parent-ruler properly. Having learned the behavior of nourishing from their mothers, the people should nourish the gentlemen (*yangjunzi* 3A3). Here, the term *yeren* (men from the wilds) is used for commoners. The agricultural fields are part of the discussion here, so that even though the emphasis is on drawing boundaries, maternal and agricultural ideas relating to nourishing are evoked, the mother with her child and the farmer with his fields and crops. The claim is that without the gentlemen, there are none to rule the people; and without the people, there are none to nourish-support-feed the gentlemen. Thus the work of the people is stated in terms of this central activity of maternal and agricultural practices, that of nourishing.

As mentioned above (in relation to 3A4), if the commoners did not learn and practice the five relations, they would be lazy, be like animals, and would eventually not even support the gentlemen. In this passage (3A3), Mencius emphasizes the "child" relation of the commoners to the superiors (the gentlemen). Thus, he says that when those above make clear the five relations, the "little" people below treat those above them as parents. Although a ruler who has become father and mother of the people cultivates his feelings, especially a maternal type of love and caretaking, it would be unacceptable to refer to the ruler as simply mother of the people. The father's authority is needed too. The mother's feelings elicit affection by the people toward the father and mother ruler, while the father's position commands obedience to patriarchal duties.

Other ancient thinkers recognized that there was something maternal-like in the behavior that the Confucians advocated, for a critic of Mencius claimed that the Confucians (*ruzhe* 儒子) praised the ancient rulers for behaving as though they were taking care of a baby (*baochizi* 保赤子, 3A5). Here we see the inversion process: the father and mother ruler takes care of the people as though they were babies; taking care of a baby is like taking care of one's aged parents (for both are weak); the children-people take care of their parents as though they were babies. Thus, in nourishing her small children, a good mother provides the model for filial sons and benevolent men. In his self-cultivation, a benevolent ruler ultimately models himself on a good mother.

King Wen is the person who best symbolizes this complex of maternal associations. In a passage that instructs men to take King Wen as their model, we see the association of King Wen, *dao*, *tian*, mothers, shame, and moral power (4A7).[7] The claim is that when *dao* (the way) prevails in the empire, those with less virtue and wisdom serve those with greater virtue and wisdom. When the way does not prevail, however, those with less power and strength serve those with greater power and strength. One must adapt to these natural circumstances (*tian*) or else risk one's destruction.

Mencius further notes with disapproval that now the small states model themselves after the big, powerful ones, and so they are ashamed at being ordered around by them. In other words, the small states do not acknowledge that their inferior positions require them to adopt a different pattern of behavior from those in a superior position. Not understanding the dynamics of behavior between strong and weak positions, the small states see their having to take orders as a matter of shame. As Mencius comments, their behavior is like that of a disciple who is ashamed of taking instructions from his teachers. Mencius' view is, of course, that there is nothing to be ashamed of in these cases, because the inferior's duty is to follow, not to command. A ruler should take King Wen as his model if he is ashamed, and if he does, he will eventually rule over the empire. Mencius supports his claim with a quote from a stanza from the *Odes* (Mao 235), saying that the descendants of Shang now serve the Zhou. Although once in the strong position, the Shang are now in the weak. It is a matter of natural circumstances (*tianming* 天命) and is not a cause for shame. Not distressed over his initially weak position, King Wen used benevolence to rule, thus enabling him to have no enemies in the empire.

In sum, ruling as father and mother of the people entails embodying the behavior of a compassionate mother as well as the behavior of filial sons and virtuous wives. The mother-wife's duties of taking care of the young and old are appropriated by the benevolent ruler in the context of the empire; they become what is essential to being a good ruler, whether he is called father and mother of the people, virtuous, or benevolent. The concept of *ren* as maternal compassion to her son is transformed into a son's filial behavior to his elderly father and these kinds of behavior are transformed into the ruler's behavior to the people. Attention to matters of timing and context is critical for success.

Chapter 8

Mothers, Feelings, and Masculinity

Maternal Compassion and Masculinity

In the Chinese philosophical tradition, Mencian ideas about the heart and moral feelings have generally been seen as part of ongoing dialogues on important Warring States issues, two interrelated ones of which concern motivation for action and the sources (internal and external) of human values and behavior. Mencius rejects the view that the ruler should be motivated by a calculation of profit and personal advantage, and he supports a position that claims a true king is motivated by natural feelings and learned behavior that is developed from those feelings. The issue of motivation is usually discussed as *yi* versus *li*, rightness versus profit, and the issue of the sources of values and behavior is seen as involving notions of *xin* (heart), *xing* (natural human tendencies, dispositions, human nature), and, in some cases, class differences.[1]

This approach to understanding Mencian thought has led to many insights, but my analysis takes another direction, as it is based on a question that has previously not been pursued in depth. The question concerns the relevance of gender to Mencian ideas about the heart or natural feelings, motivation, and behavior. My claim is that Mencius advocates a certain masculine ideal, embodied in the true king, and that this ideal form of masculinity incorporates gender traits widely accepted as female. As he promotes his views, he must suppress awareness of this similarity with femininity (because of possible feelings of anxiety and shame) and reassure men that this new behavior is much more effective than the aggressive type. Assuming that humans have various types of inborn feelings that can be developed in behavior or quashed, just as seeds can grow to become mature plants or stunted plants or never even germinate,

Mencius is especially interested in identifying those particular feelings that, if developed, will help a man became a gentleman, who is none other than the ruler who is father and mother of the people and a filial son within his family.

The Mencian conception of the heart (one's spontaneous feelings) is central to the processes of transformation described in previous chapters, for the heart is deemed the source both of maternal feelings and practices and of patriarchal virtues and social order. These two kinds of practices, maternal and patriarchal, are not a theoretical pair and are not equally recognized in the text, for only the latter is the subject of Mencian thought. As argued above, the political practices of a father and mother ruler are a transformation of the practices of filial piety, which in turn are a transformation of maternal practices. The discussion now turns to the four feelings (hearts), also conceived as the four beginnings and, as we shall see, in other ways as well.

Discussed by many scholars, the Mencian claim is that the four beginnings or feelings are the foundation of (patriarchal) social values and order. The fact that the relevant feelings are four in number and are correlated with four cornerstone social values reflects the results of efforts to categorize and systematize human traits and behavior.[2] The Mencian position thus represents a statement of beliefs already partially developed, rather than a tentative initial hypothesis. Moreover, the fact that Mencius directly attempts to demonstrate the existence of only one of the natural feelings suggests that that feeling is somehow pivotal. This feeling is what Mencius calls *ceyinzhixin* 惻隱之心 (2A6, 6A6), a term that suggests feelings of commiseration, pity, sympathy, compassion, and pain and distress from the suffering of others. I translate it here as compassion, but we need to keep in mind that it actually refers to a set of interrelated feelings, not just one.

At least one of the many reasons for the importance of compassion is that in Chinese culture both human and animal mothers were assumed to have natural feelings of compassion and concern for their babies. The most successful nurturing practices of humans in taking care of babies and small children no doubt contributed to this belief, and even the successful behavior of mothers among animals was interpreted as an indication of caring. That compassion is the core feeling is further suggested by use of the particular term "the heart that cannot endure [the suffering of] others" (*burenrenzhixin* 不忍人之心, 2A6) to refer to the four feelings as a whole. Suffering was especially associated with women, as the following discussion will bring out, and both terms, compassion and the heart that cannot endure [the suffering of] others, have a root meaning of suffering with. In contrast to the ruthless feelings and behavior attributed to men who were warriors and hunters, it is not unlikely that some notion of a genuinely caring heart was attributed to the maternal feelings and behavior of women at home. Mencius, however, was theorizing that the maternal good heart was a heart that men, too, all have (*renjieyouzhi* 人皆有之, 6A6).

I make this hypothesis based in part on a critical difference between the feeling of compassion (*ceyinzhixin*) and the other three feelings—shame and dislike (of shameful behavior) (*xiuwuzhixin* 羞惡之心), deference and modesty (*cirangzhixin* 辭讓之心; or respect *gongjingzhixin* 敬恭之心), and approving (the appropriate or right thing to do) and disapproving (the inappropriate or wrong thing to do) (*shifeizhixin* 是非之心). Like compassion, these terms suggest sets of interrelated feelings. However, passages in many texts suggest a widespread belief that compassion can and does occur in settings outside the political state and society, whereas the other three feelings require society and social norms. That is, in feeling compassion and in behaving compassionately, one need not recognize social boundaries of any kind, either among humans or between humans and animals. Genuine compassion simply flows outward, erasing or not recognizing boundaries. This characteristic makes compassion both dangerous and important to social order. It can weaken the boundaries that in Mencian thought help construct society and its social ordering in the face of the wild natural world of animals, plants, and rivers, and it can motivate people to maintain those boundaries.

In contrast to the positive overflowing of compassion, shame is closely associated with an unwanted overflowing of boundaries.[3] To feel shame requires that one recognize boundaries and accept their validity in some way. Shame is especially (and often implicitly) linked to certain activities of women—menstruation, childbirth, and blood, in Chinese and other cultures. Like social disobedience, these things are considered potentially dangerous and evil, and they indicate a lack of self-control. In addition, Mencian thought holds that those who are social inferiors often lack sufficient self-control and so are likely to behave in a wild manner. Shame is thus closely linked to women as both mothers and wives, as well as to others who are seen to be in need of regulation. Men who value a more martial and aggressive type of masculinity do not want their behavior to be seen as similar to that of women, and they feel shame if it is. They see shame, like compassion, as female gendered behavior.

In taking care of their children and their husband's parents, mothers and wives have no choice but to engage in behavior that can be and is interpreted as deferential or yielding. Such women must respond to children's needs if the children are to survive, and in meeting the needs of babies and children, a mother often must put their needs before her own. Mothers must learn to understand that the needs of children change as they grow, and so successful caretaking practices also reflect a yielding to changing conditions. The wife's responsibilities to her parents-in-law are similarly shaped by feelings and patterns of deference, as are those of men in subordinate positions. Thus deference also is strongly associated with female gendered behavior.

In taking care of their children, mothers constantly must make choices about appropriate and inappropriate actions. It is assumed that they naturally prefer what is appropriate, since that is associated with success in child rearing. This feeling of knowing and approving of the right thing to do in a particular situation takes place within a larger context of competing interests. It is similar to the concept of situational weighing or adaptive behavior (*quan* 權), which is central to both maternal and farming practices and is important in Confucian-Mencian moral and political thinking. For those with little or less power in society, such as wives and men in subordinate positions, survival may well depend upon how well they can develop this ability (discussed below).

My hypothesis then is that certain spontaneous feelings and the behavior resulting from the expression of these feelings is culturally conceived as naturally belonging to mothers and to women as wives. Such feelings and their related behavior are considered female gendered. At the same time, Mencius, like some others before him, opposes the ruthless and aggressive behavior of rulers, although many people implicitly consider that kind of behavior as the masculine ideal. In formulating his political philosophy, which concerns the behavior of men, Mencius thus proposes a different ideal of masculinity, one that rejects ruthless and cruel behavior and incorporates elements of the compassionate and cooperative behavior of women in the family. His is more a *wen* 文 (cultural) type of masculinity, as opposed to a *wu* 武 (martial) type.[4] Mencius systematizes the supposedly female gendered feelings into a set of four good ones and correlates them with a set of four virtues in (patriarchal) society. Addressing men, especially elite men, Mencius is applying the virtues and their inborn beginnings to men, thus promoting a new kind of masculine behavior. This then is, in brief, the context of his claim that men too have these feelings (this heart).

If my hypothesis is valid, we can then grasp just how politically significant and risky Mencius' instructions to the king are, that is, his instructions to be compassionate and to be a father and mother to the people.

Through implicit linkages of associations, Mencius is instructing the ruler and all males to practice certain kinds of female gendered behavior. But to do so is considered shameful by many and not fully masculine. However, the Mencian position has its strengths. It offers rulers a way to maintain patriarchal hierarchy and order and to continue to use force when deemed necessary. A large, agriculturally based society, with an expanding economy and population, provides many situations in which occupational, class, and gender distinctions are easily blurred. Such blurring not only is believed to be a basis of social-political disorder, it eventually raises questions about beliefs in fundamental differences between men and women. Although force is used to maintain distinctions and order, increasingly it is not sufficient by itself. Thus, if men and women can be seen as sharing some of the same traits, as alike in some ways, then those traits that are conducive to obedience, yielding, sympathy, and cooperation can be developed as an ideal in men, just as in women. If these traits are inborn, moreover, his position is even stronger. The Mencian position is fraught with difficulties and danger, however, for it is trying both to maintain some distinctions and to erase others, and the results of such efforts have seldom turned out to be controllable.

In the full Mencian elaboration of the theory of the heart, the four feelings (beginnings, sprouts) are linked to certain elite male gendered virtues that are to be developed in the context of the patriarchal social order, namely, benevolence (*ren*), rightness (*yi*), ritual propriety (*li*), and wisdom (*zhi*). Learning is understood here as involving the development of what one already possesses, like a seed's development into a plant, rather than as something imposed on one from outside. The development of these virtues thus occurs according to a type of biological and maternal process, characterized by a pattern of birth, nourishment, cultivation, and growth. The resulting type of society is the strongest society, for it is based on the patterns of the cosmos itself.

In addition to the text's references to the practices and work of women (mothers and wives) and to practices of farming, the passages about the heart thus provide further evidence of a tacit maternal basis to Mencian thinking about masculinity. Such passages relate directly to the concept of the benevolent (father and mother) ruler, which requires that one must first be a filial son. The most important passages that speak about the heart, directly or indirectly, are 2A2.1–23, 2A6, 4A17, 4A27, 1A7, 6A6, 7A15, and 7A26. None of the original conversations speak directly about the heart as the four feelings, but many are concerned with the virtuous behavior that can be developed from these four or from other feelings. For instance, we see benevolence and rightness in 1A1, filial piety, fraternal deference, loyalty, and good faith in 1A5, enjoyment in 1B1, and affection in 1B12, all of which are passages among the original Mencius interviews.

Discussing the Heart

Mencius' discussion of the heart begins with his discussion of courage (*yong* 勇), for courage is absolutely necessary to achieving the kind of masculinity that he advocates. From the second layer of the text, the passage on courage, or the "heart that cannot be stirred [to fear]" (*budongxin* 不動心, 2A2), is also the earliest to examine moral feelings (the heart) in a theoretical way. The importance of being straight (*suo* 縮) or true to one's spontaneous feelings, a condition that one can know by self-examination, is made clear here. Like the English word courage, which derives from the Latin word "cor," meaning heart, spirit, mind, the Mencian concept of courage is also centrally concerned with the *xin* (heart, mind, feelings, spirit). Like the other feelings, courage suggests a set of interrelated feelings that include not being fearful, anxious, worried, scared, or terrified. Mencius' view is, in effect, that a man of genuine courage does not become fearful when he is facing a dangerous, difficult, or painful situation, even if that situation entails behaving in a radically new way. Such a person cannot be made fearful because his actions are true to his natural feelings of compassion.

In response to the question of how one can attain a steadfast or unwavering heart, Mencius offers three ways of how specific men cultivated or nourished their courage (*yangyong*). The first man responded with the same kind of fierceness to everyone and every situation, making no distinctions regarding social position or degree of threat. Recognizing that the outcome of a conflict cannot be known in advance, the second man decided that all he could do was to make sure he himself had no fear. Of these two, Mencius believes that the second has a better, but still not full, grasp of what is essential to courage, since he engages in some self-cultivation. The third man's method, that of Zengzi, was to make sure that upon self-examination he was straight (*suo*) or true. If he were not, he would fear even a common man in coarse clothing. But if he were true, he would have no fear going against thousands of men.

Zengzi's method receives the full approval of Mencius because Zengzi protects and preserves that which is essential. Using the second method, Meng Shishe only protects his *qi* (*qi* has many meanings but here refers to one's bodily energy and activity). One cannot alleviate feelings of anxiety and fear, however, by looking to one's *qi* for help. Whether fierce or compliant, one's actions may disguise but will not eliminate fear, for fear is an involuntary feeling. We may not talk about such kinds of feelings or even be able to put them into words, and we may try to deny or disguise them, but such actions will not eradicate them. To eradicate feelings like fear and anxiety, Mencius' view is that one must cultivate one's other types of natural, spontaneous feelings, in particular, the four beginnings. In claiming here that he understands words, Mencius is thus saying that he understands how words and actions may or may not be true to one's inborn spontaneous feelings.

Mencius goes on to say that one's aspirations (*zhi* 志) are the commander (*shuai* 率) of one's *qi*, which is what fills up the body. Like other feelings, the notion (feeling) of aspirations suggests not just one but a set of feelings that includes hopes, aims, and desires to achieve what is good. Feelings, it should be emphasized, are natural and involuntary. They are not the result of calculation, rationalization, or other forms of conscious and deliberate thinking. Thus, *zhi* has the opposite meaning of intentions or the will, which are common translations. In Mencius' view, feelings are the original sources of one's behavior, whether one knows it consciously or not. They motivate one to act even if they or their link to behavior is not in one's awareness. In this passage Mencius uses *zhi* (aspirations) interchangeably with *xin* (heart, feelings); so his claim is that one's aspirations or one's original feelings stimulate and push forward one's behavior. Although one's heart (feelings) and *qi* affect each other, one's heart is ultimately that which motivates one to do what is good. Therefore, one must support and maintain one's aspirations, for they are primary, but still one must not harm one's *qi*. Mencius does not deny the thinking actions of the heart, but they are not the issue here in this discussion on courage.

Elsewhere, Mencius phrases this effort and tension in a slightly different way, stating that one must make the right distinctions between what is more valuable and less valuable in a given context. Using familiar examples, Mencius compares the distinction between the greater lesser and lesser parts of one's body with that between the valuable and common trees of a gardener (6A14). He emphasizes that by standing firmly in one's greater part (the heart's functioning), one's lesser parts (the body's functioning) cannot steal one's inborn feelings (6A15).

Considering the gender dimensions of this conversation so far, we see that the concepts and types of behavior mentioned have strong associations with military matters and a type of masculine behavior exhibited in a military action. The above examples of how three men cultivated their courage are set in contexts that suggest conflicts and battle. The words regarding behavior—protect and preserve (*shou* 守), support and maintain (*chi* 持), and commander (*shuai*), are military terms. Both the contexts of action and the terms used clearly apply to male practices. At the same time, Mencius also uses terms that derive from women's practices and so have tacit feminine associations. The term used here for straight or true, which is part of Zengzi's method, is *suo*, which originally meant the straight seams from the top to the edge of a man's cap.[5] This term thus contains a tacit reference to sewing, which is women's work. To nourish or cultivate is closely connected to maternal actions of feeding and taking care of babies, that is, what is small and in need of help.

Thus, in explaining courage, or an unwavering heart, a trait that applies to male behavior, and how to nourish it, Mencius employs three sets of associations, two masculine and one feminine. Aspirations, commander, heart, courage, self-reflection, and ruling are included in a favorable set of masculine associations that is contrasted, explicitly and implicitly, to an unfavorable masculine set of *qi*, follower, fear, rashness, compliance, and inferior men. Sewing, nourishing, the heart, and feelings all are linked to women's behavior.

This passage helps to construct Mencius' ideal masculinity in the following way. Mencius assumes that, given the models of several kinds of masculinity, men will choose the type most associated with courage and commanding, because they see this type as most masculine. Mencius shows, however, that this more military type of masculine behavior is actually a lesser type, because it is linked to fear, rashness, and mere *qi*. A better type is the kind he advocates. For cultural reasons such as shame, however, people do not want to acknowledge its link to female behavior. The use of these sets of overlapping associations helps Mencius suppress the female connection. That is, since feelings and the heart belong to Mencius' conceptions of courage and masculinity, their link to maternal compassion can be ignored.

As the dialogue continues in 2A2, Mencius expands on how to nourish one's courage and so attain this ultimate state in which a man is not troubled by feelings of anxiety, fear, conflict, and shame. It is comparable to that state of being described by Confucius as following what his heart desired (i. e., his cultivated good feelings) without going beyond what is appropriate (*Lunyu* 2.4). Using *qi* in a special sense and indicating how he nourishes his courage, Mencius says that he (himself) is good at nourishing his flood-like *qi* (*haoranzhiqi* 浩然之氣).[6] He explains that as a type of *qi* it is the greatest and the strongest. If one nourishes it by being true to one's incipient good feelings and one does not harm it, the moral behavior resulting from its development will pervade the world. More specifically, as a type of *qi* it assists one in developing appropriate and moral behavior, and if one does not develop it into moral behavior, one starves it. It grows from acts of rightness accumulated over time; its cultivation is not achieved by occasional displays of rightness. Moreover, if one's behavior does not bring one genuine feelings of joy, satisfaction, and peace, then one starves one's flood-like *qi*.

Therefore, one should serve it with appropriate behavior but not make it one's focus. One should not forget about it in one's thoughts and feelings, but one should also not (inappropriately) help it to grow. One should not behave like the man from Song who helped his sprouts of grain to grow by pulling them up, thus causing them to wither and die. Mencius further says that although some men do not weed their sprouts at all, most are like the man from Song. Mencius emphasizes with this and other examples that one must not only make the effort to nourish one's moral sprouts, but one must make the right kind of effort. Otherwise one's sprouts will die and bad behavior will be the result.

Mencius does claim, moreover, that all men have the capability to make the effort. Using terms that appear only in the last layer of the text, the Mencian position is that all men naturally have both spontaneous moral feelings (*liangzhi*) and the abilities (*liangneng*) to develop them into the virtues of society (7A15). Mencius presents this view in several passages, one of which is a separate conversation with the ruler in which Mencius claims that the ruler is able to behave morally but he fails to make the effort (1A7). He claims that behaving morally is no more difficult than lifting a feather or viewing a load of firewood. That such things do not happen is simply due to one's not making the effort.

The idea of lifting a feather is a powerful cultural image used previously in relation to this sagely form of masculinity. In the sixth stanza of the *Odes*, Mao 260, partially quoted in 6A6 and referred to below, a popular saying is quoted that evokes the image of lifting a feather. Referring to a man's making the effort to behave morally and actually behaving so, this stanza says that one's virtue or inward power (*de*) is as light as a feather but only Zhong Shanfu can lift it.[7] In this way Mencius thus suggests that physical strength is not the issue in genuine masculine behavior.

In explaining further what he means by spontaneous moral feelings and knowledge (*liangzhi*) and the natural abilities (*liangneng*) to develop them, Mencius states that what a man can do without learning is his natural good ability, and what he can feel and know without pondering is his natural good knowledge (7A15). To support this claim, Mencius says that all babies and little boys know to love (*ai*) their parents (*qin*), and when grown, they all know to respect (*jing*) their older brothers. To treat your parents properly and affectionately (*qinqin*) is benevolence; to respect your elders (*jingzhang*) is rightness. Echoing the advice given to the ruler previously (1A7), Mencius concludes that there is nothing else to do but to extend this kind of behavior to the empire.

The male gendering of this behavior is indicated by the concern with the two critical relations of the five relations, that of father and son and of older and younger brother, and the message is addressed to the ruler because only he is in a position to oversee the empire. (I translate *qin* as parents here, instead of father, because of the mention of babies and little boys, who are associated with mothers.) As in 4A27 and other passages, this passage groups together terms for filial piety and terms for fraternal deference, and it defines benevolence and rightness as filial piety and fraternal deference. Small children (young boys) are different from sons and younger brothers. They do not fit into any of the five relations, and their behavior is seen as still unshaped by society. Their behavior is still closely associated with their mothers. Thus the implication of *aiqin* (loving one's parents) differs significantly from filial piety, benevolence, and treating parents properly and affectionately, which combine one's inborn feelings with cultivation and learning. The fact that babies and little children are said to have inborn feelings and knowledge and inborn abilities makes mothers closely associated with these spontaneous traits because of the close association of mothers and babies.

In addition, as a further look at the above conversation about developing courage by nourishing one's flood-like *qi* indicates, Mencius conceives his overflowing, flood-like *qi* in terms of imagery related to both plants and females. The overflowing *qi* is, in effect, another term that Mencius uses to talk about the four feelings or sprouts, the heart, or one's incipient and spontaneous moral feelings. All these terms refer to the same human phenomenon, which as Mencius admits is difficult to explain in words. Drawing on knowledge familiar to most people, Mencius compares his overflowing *qi* to young sprouts that are just beginning to germinate. One also has to nourish them constantly and carefully. One cannot force them to grow or completely ignore them, for such actions will eventually kill them.

Moral behavior and its beginnings must be cultivated in the same way if they are to reach full development. Success in nourishing one's flood-like *qi*, one's incipient moral feelings, leads not only to practicing moral behavior externally but also to attaining that unwavering heart internally. This latter term describes a state in which a man feels and is genuinely courageous; he is truly free from fear, anxiety, and other such feelings that in Mencius' view lead to harmful governmental practices and the kind of masculinity that he rejects.

The necessity to nourish, constantly take care of, not let starve, and not use inappropriate methods with one's overflowing *qi* indicates a fundamental association of moral behavior with female, especially maternal, practices, as well as with farming practices. Clear recognition of this association with female gendered behavior is not acceptable, and so it is resisted by the inclusion of the uncontrollable dimensions of women along with their nourishing and life-giving dimensions. Vast, overflowing, flooding waters are associated with disorder, the lack of boundaries, danger, shame, and females. Thus the very designation of this kind of *qi* as flood-like serves both to enable one to recognize that the origins of morality and moral sprouts are widely regarded as female related and then to forget that one has ever recognized this association. One needs to forget because of the danger to society of women's perceived uncontrollability. In effect, one's overflowing *qi* and *liangzhi* are equivalent to the four feelings or four sprouts, but without the specificity of their systematization. Having established the importance of courage, Mencius can then explain what he means by the heart and its link to his masculine ideal.

Philosophical theorizing about the heart's spontaneous moral feelings occurs most fully in two sections of the text, 2A6 (third layer) and 6A (sixth layer), which present similar accounts of the four beginnings along with some differences in argumentation, terms, and concepts. Mencius appeals to various analogies, but his use of plant related imagery always enables tacit associations with feminine behavior to remain. His position has six fundamental aspects:

(1) The beginnings of moral feelings and behavior are inborn, natural, involuntary, and spontaneous.

(2) These inborn feelings are characteristic of men as well as women.

(3) They are characteristic of all men regardless of the obviously bad behavior of some.

(4) One needs to make deliberate and careful efforts to develop them if they are to be reflected in one's behavior and not lost.

(5) Their full development will result in the flourishing of a humane society.

(6) There is no shame for a man to cultivate these sprouts of morality, even though people associate them with feminine behavior. Rather, achieving this great masculinity absolutely requires courage.

Mencius begins with the claim (in 2A6) that all men have this heart that cannot endure [the suffering of] others. Supporting this position by appealing to the authority of the ancient sages, he states that the former kings had this heart (these feelings) and consequently their governments had this characteristic too. That is, they cultivated and put into practice their incipient moral feelings. Moreover, it is very easy to rule the empire when one uses this heart to implement such a government. By mentioning the former kings, Mencius gives support to his claim that all men have this heart, but without a second assumption, that all men are alike, the argument remains quite weak. This assumption is stated, however, in several places.

At the end of Mencius' discussion on courage (in 2A2), the issue of sagehood is raised, with Mencius' insisting that Confucius is the foremost sage among sages and is his model. The phenomenon of one entity's emerging as superior to all others of the same type does not just apply to men (*min*), moreover. Animals, birds, hills, and waters all have their own examples of the superior one among them. Thus, just as the unicorn is the same in kind as other animals, the phoenix as other birds, Taishan as other mounds and hills, and the rivers and the sea as other streams and rain ponds, so the sage (Confucius) and men (*min*) are the same in kind. Using plant related imagery to describe how the superior one emerges from others of its kind and rises up from the thick fields, Mencius claims that no one has flourished more than Confucius. Elsewhere Mencius also indicates that all men are the same in kind by citing his approval of the views of Shun, who believed that goodness is the same in men (2A8), and by arguing (in 6A7) that the preferences of men's various senses are all the same.

To illustrate that all men, not just the sages, have this heart (these feelings) that cannot endure the suffering of others, Mencius gives the example of a child about to fall into a well. Mencius claims that upon seeing this, all men naturally and spontaneously have feelings of fear and alarm (*chuti* 怵惕), pain and commiseration (*ceyin*). These feelings do not arise from some hidden motive, such as wanting to gain the parents' favor or the praise of others, or wanting to make a show of compassion for fear of gaining a reputation of not caring.[8]

By using as his example the misfortune of a child, who is not to be confused with a son in the father and son relation, Mencius openly appeals to a set of associations that include children, mothers, suffering, and compassion. Children are vulnerable, unable to take care of themselves, and so must rely on their mother's compassion, which is believed to be spontaneously given and not based on ulterior motives. Had Mencius used some other example, such as a strong, adult man, not related to children, Mencius' claim would not have worked as it did. The argument works because it is already believed that mothers have natural and spontaneous feelings of compassion as they take care of their babies and young children. Now the claim is that men have these sprouts of compassion too. Moreover, since all men have them, even those rulers who are criticized by Mencius as ruthless also have these inborn feelings. Thus, they can change their behavior if they want to do so.

Mencius then claims that just as one is not a man without this feeling (heart) of compassion, one also is not a man without the feelings of shame and dislike, deference, and approval and disapproval. He further claims that these four feelings are the beginnings (*duan* 端) respectively of the four virtues of benevolence, rightness, ritual action, and wisdom. To support this position, Mencius argues first that men have these four beginnings just as they have four limbs. Then, for rhetorical effect, he says that if a man denies that he or his ruler can help his own sprouts to grow, he is simply stealing from himself or his ruler.

Mencius finishes his argument by pointing out that, since they all have these four beginnings within themselves, men should know that if they develop them fully, the result will be irrepressible like a fire beginning to blaze forth or like a spring bubbling up. Returning to the critical issue of compassion, Mencius then claims that if a man, that is, a ruler, is able to develop fully his four beginnings, they will enable him (as the ruler) to care for and protect (*bao*) all within the four seas. But if he does not develop them, they will not enable him even to serve his father and mother. Psychological to the core, his argument is bolstered by the evocation of, and implicit comparison with, these persuasive images.

The Mencian position is, in effect, that a benevolent ruler will be able to act like a mother in caring for, loving, and protecting her infant. Mencius recognizes in some way, however, that advocating a type of masculinity that recognizes and cultivates compassion is culturally unacceptable because such behavior is considered shameful for men. Although in other situations they are linked to females, here the images of a fire and a spring help to make recognition of the association with women avoidable by focusing attention away from mothers. The comparison to a mother's feeling of compassion is further obscured by transferring the site from the mother and child relationship to that of the ruler and ruled within the empire. This latter site entails the new Mencian relation of the father and mother ruler and the children-people. The maternal association is still not fully buried, however, for it is claimed that if a ruler does not develop his moral beginnings, he will not even be able to be a filial son toward his parents, that is, serve his father and mother.

Mencius employs other approaches as well in addressing the issue of shame. One is that he makes sharp distinctions between his model of masculinity and the one he is opposing, and he emphasizes the deficiency of the latter. For instance, the ruler who follows his model behaves like Kings Tang and Wen, who ruled with virtue and so gained men's submission voluntarily. In contrast, the hegemon rules with force and never gains the voluntary submission of men (2A3). Men can thus better understand how their own behavior differs from Mencius' ideal.

In a related way Mencius emphasizes that a gentleman is responsible for his own actions and choices and he cannot blame others for his own lack of success. He claims that if a man's behavior is not characterized by benevolence, wisdom, ritual propriety, and rightness, then he is just making himself into a servant of others (2A7). Then, to be ashamed of being a servant is like a bow maker's or an arrow maker's being ashamed of making bows or arrows. Thus a man has to select his type of work carefully. Moreover, practicing moral behavior is similar to shooting an arrow. If a man misses the target, he does not blame others, but seeks the reason in himself.

Another approach is his use of positive models such as Shun and King Wen, who are foremost exemplars of compassion and benevolence. Another positive model is Zhong Shanfu, who is not cited by name but is described in one passage from the *Odes* from which Mencius quotes and is undoubtedly well known to all who are familiar with the *Odes*. In Mao 260 in the stanza following the one quoted by Mencius (in 6A6), Zhong Shanfu's virtues are described in terms that include both female and male gender traits. On the one hand, his (feminine type of) behavior was mild (*rou* 柔, soft) and admirable (*jia* 嘉), holding fast to the norms, cautious and composed, and he did not take advantage of the helpless and weak (those without wives or husbands). On the other hand, reflecting traditional masculine behavior, his deportment and appearance were noble and commanding, he was given the king's charge to be a model to all the officers, he did not fear those who were strong and oppressive, his horses were powerful, and he was in charge of military operations. Zhong Shanfu was not a ruler, but he was a prominent military official, and like Kings Wen and Wu he embodied the virtues of the Mencian ideal of masculinity. Some of the virtues were widely recognized as masculine and others generally perceived as feminine. The former included military and political leadership, as well as a certain personal demeanor, and the latter entailed those that were considered soft, such as kindness and obedience. Mencius thus emphasizes that this model of masculinity is certainly not a cause for shame.

A similar approach is to cite examples of this type of masculine behavior that served to reassure men that if they behaved this way, they were not really like a woman. For instance, in one conversation the king reveals that he was unable to bear seeing the fear and trembling, that is, the suffering, of the ox and so he substituted a sheep instead (1A7). The sheep (possibly a lamb) not seen was smaller than the ox and so people thought he made the exchange because of the smaller expense. Mencius points out, however, that a gentleman cannot bear to see animals die or eat their meat once he has seen them alive or heard their crying, and so he keeps himself away from the butchering site and kitchen. And the king's practice of compassion is similar. In other words, behaving according to the Mencian ideal of masculinity still keeps men at a distance from women, who are represented here by the kitchen, a site of women's work. Although Mencius does not say it, his message is in effect that a man should not be ashamed of behaving compassionately and deferentially like a woman, but should be ashamed of not behaving in this way.

A further approach is his emphasis on the feelings of pleasure, delight, and joy that this sagely form of masculinity brings. For instance, Mencius states that benevolence is fulfilled in serving one's father, rightness in following one's older brother, wisdom in understanding and holding onto these two virtues, ritual propriety in regulating and adorning the practice of these two virtues, and music in delighting in the practice of these two virtues (4A27). When one delights in these practices, these virtues grow and cannot be stopped. And without even realizing it, one's hands and feet are moving and dancing. Although it is not stated openly, this description of the joy a man will feel from this highest form of masculine behavior is an argument against possible feelings of shame and anxiety.

As he continues to argue that all men too have these spontaneous moral feelings, Mencius gives attention to competing views of human tendencies or dispositions and emphasizes other aspects of his own position, especially those requiring thought and deliberation. He highlights the constant struggle between external destructive conditions and one's own efforts at cultivation (6A7, 6A8). He stresses the necessity of fully concentrating one's efforts (6A9) and making the right choices so as not to lose one's original feelings (6A10). His focus further turns to the need for reflection, for making proper distinctions, and for recognizing what is more and what is less important (6A11–17).

Using slightly different terms that result in minimizing the explicit references to feelings, Mencius argues with Gaozi about whether one's *xing* (natural tendencies or dispositions) are internally or externally derived (6A1–4). Gaozi's view is that a man's natural tendencies or dispositions do not have preferences that inherently shape his behavior. Rather, one's natural tendencies or dispositions are similar to such things as willow trees and swirling water, while benevolence and rightness are similar to cups and bowls made from the wood and the multiple directions in which water can flow. Mencius counters with the points that the tree must be destroyed to make cups and bowls and that water's natural tendency is to flow downward. Thus it makes no sense to promote good behavior if that behavior results in destroying people. Moreover, water does have a natural preference, for it is well known that water will naturally flow down, not up, although it may flow east or west.

Although the focus is slightly different between those who argue about men's natural tendencies or dispositions (*xing*) and Mencius, who is talking about men's spontaneous feelings (*xin*), Mencius makes clear how his views relate to those concerned with *xing*. Suggesting developments in philosophical discourse, new terms appear in these later conversations, including *xing*, *qing* 情 (feelings), and *cai* 才 (natural abilities). Arguing against several different conceptions of *xing*, Mencius maintains that a man's *xing* is good. Moreover, what he specifically means by that claim is that a man's inborn spontaneous feelings (*qing*) are good. One's failure to behave morally is not the fault of one's natural abilities (*cai*) but is due to other factors. Although *qing* has other meanings, here Mencius uses the term *qing* in the sense of *xin*, meaning feelings. With a slight change in wording but not in overall meaning from 2A6, Mencius reiterates that all men have feelings (*xin*) of compassion, shame, respect (*gongjing*), and of approval and disapproval. When developed, these feelings lead respectively to benevolence, rightness, ritual propriety, and wisdom. Thus these virtues are not welded onto one from outside but are possessed naturally. Nonetheless, one still must work at developing them, or they will be lost (6A6).[9]

As he did with the illustration involving the child and the well, Mencius defends his position by appealing to an example that works because of implicit cultural beliefs. Here he cites a passage from the *Odes* and Confucius' approval of its claim. The stanza (Mao 260) states that *tian* gave birth to the people and to the norms by which things are constituted.[10] In other words, the cultural and physiological traits of men are rooted in the natural conditions of the world (*tian*). The ode further says that when the people hold onto their constant dispositions, they love these beautiful feminine virtues (*yide* 懿德). I translate *yide* as beautiful feminine virtues because the term implies women's virtues, which are considered admirable and beautiful, although other translators do not bring out the feminine association.[11] Here, *tian* also appropriates the birth function of mothers, for this stanza says that *tian* gave birth to the people and to Zhong Shanfu. (The second half of this stanza is not quoted here.) Similar to the illustration of the child and the well, this example used by Mencius to support his position has implicit maternal associations.

Aware of objections to his views and having already attempted to counter some of them, Mencius addresses the issue of bad behavior by emphasizing that it is often due to external circumstances, not inborn traits (6A7). Putting aside the matter of effort here, to make his case that the differences among men's behavior are due to circumstances, he gives the examples of sons and younger brothers in good versus bad harvest years, of barley's growing under different conditions, and of feet, for which shoes are made. The young men, he points out, are mostly good in the years when the harvest is successful but bad when the harvest fails. The difference is not due to their natural abilities (*cai*), but rather to what entraps their hearts (feelings). Similarly, the differences in crops of barley are due to differences in the richness of the soil, the amount of rainfall and moisture, and human efforts—and not to the barley itself. And feet are all the same shape, although they differ in size.

To strengthen his position, Mencius returns again to his claim that these ideas apply to everyone since all men are alike. His argument here for the similarity of all men is that everyone has the same preferences in regard to the sensory experiences of tasting, hearing, and seeing. The same is true of the heart and its activities of feeling and thinking, and *li* (patterns) and *yi* (rightness) are what one's heart approves of.[12] Given the discussion throughout the text and the sensory comparisons here, I take *li* and *yi* as abstractions for the virtues developed from the inborn feelings. The idea is that one's heart prefers the virtues developed from one's spontaneous moral sprouts, just as one's mouth prefers good tastes, one's ears prefer harmonious music, and one's eyes prefer beautiful sights.

The issue of shame for men behaving in this Mencian way, which some see as less masculine, remains as an unspoken subtext here. Thus, in this passage Mencius also tacitly affirms that you as a man will not be ashamed if you behave in this sagely way. Such behavior will bring you pleasure, not shame, and you are not behaving like a woman. Mencius presents this message indirectly by the examples he uses, as well as by openly stating that *li* and *yi* please his heart. The person chosen to represent beauty is a man, Zidu, who is also known for his treachery, and the person chosen as the connoisseur of good tastes is Yiya, an extremely skillful cook, who is also known for his moral laxity. These examples help prevent recognition of a female association with this proposed kind of masculinity because they are men. At the same time, however, the female link is not completely obliterated, since women are often associated with immorality and are often considered obstacles to a man's cultivating his moral behavior. Although Yiya and Zidu are men, they are considered immoral and so implicitly like women.

To help men avoid recognizing the association of feminine gender traits with Mencius' sagely type of masculinity, women had to be distanced from this masculine moral behavior. Mencius employs various methods to achieve this distancing (including the teaching of the separation of functions between husband and wife), and here his method is to offer examples of competing choices. Given the choice between rightness and life itself, the nonmoral choice is associated with women, either directly or indirectly. For instance, although obtaining some rice and soup, which are linked to women through feeding, means that a man can stay alive rather than die from starvation, they are the wrong choice if offered in an insulting way, even to someone starving (6A10). Ritual propriety is more important. In addition, a man's improper acceptance of ten thousand bushels of grain in order to enjoy beautiful mansions, the services of wives and concubines, and the gratitude of needy acquaintances also shows that he has lost his original heart (*benxin* 本心). Here, his nonmoral behavior is clearly linked to women. Making a choice in these kinds of situation is termed *quan* (situational weighing).

Adding to his arguments that a man's presently bad behavior is no reason for assuming that he did not originally have moral feelings, Mencius turns to an analogy with Ox Mountain (6A8). The mountain once had lush growth, but it is now bare because day after day its trees were chopped down and its plants were overgrazed. The mountain's constant attempts to regrow its sprouts were outpaced by the axes and cattle. The same is true with men. They all have a heart of benevolence and rightness, a good heart (*liangxin*), but they lose their innately good feelings in the same way.[13] Eventually the constantly harsh and destructive circumstances of their lives cause their spontaneous moral feelings to lose their beauty and die. Using language associated with plants, growth, nourishment, and so also mothers, Mencius claims all things will grow if given proper nourishment, but if that nourishment is denied, they will wither and die. If a man does not tend his moral feelings, he will resemble the wild animals.

From these statements and arguments of Mencius, we can see how the maternal associations are woven into his ideas in a fundamental way. Despite the masking of links among women's behavior (femininity), spontaneous moral feelings, and masculinity in these ways, references to the body and to plants, and to the need to make an effort, to focus one's efforts, and to cultivate oneself all result in a constant returning to the grounding of these ideas in the farming and maternal contexts.

Use of the concept of situational weighing (*quan*) is a further aspect of Mencius' approach in arguing against those who oppose his position and for addressing issues of masculinity. By bringing attention to the deficiencies in the kinds of male behavior that he opposes, his examples demonstrate that his conception of male behavior is preferable. The term *quan* (variously translated as situational weighing, using discretion, using appropriate judgment, not being rigid in holding to a standard, adaptive behavior, exigency) actually appears, in this sense, in only a few passages, but other passages speak about same issue.

One well-known passage (4A17) is concerned with the conflict between letting someone die by rigidly following ritual propriety and saving that person's life by violating the norms. Here, ritual propriety entails that males and females do not touch each other, but the situation is that a man's sister-in-law is drowning. Violating ritual, he can save her by extending his hand to her, or he can follow ritual and let her drown. Mencius' view is that he should save her. To let her die would be to behave like wolves, whose behavior Mencius implicitly compares to that of ruthless rulers.

In another passage (7A26) Mencius evaluates the views of Yangzi, Mozi, and Zimo, and while he sees Zimo as better than Yangzi and Mozi because of his centrist position, Zimo is still criticized because he is rigid in holding to a single point. His rigidity reflects his inability to use discretion (*quan*), thus suggesting feelings of anxiety and possibly fear. Mencius rejects Yang Zhu's selfishness because it completely denies one's spontaneous moral feelings, especially that of compassion, and the virtues developed from them. Although Mo Di's advocacy of universal love may seem to be similar to Mencius' thinking about compassion, universal love denies the virtues, which are the fruit of the development of compassion and the other spontaneous feelings. Mo Di and Mencius use the same terms, such as *ren* and *yi*, but give them different meanings.

In a further illustration, Mencius reminds the ruler that people know what's light and what's heavy by weighing and what's long and what's short by measuring (1A7). The ruler should do the same with his heart and government, that is, examine how his policies relate to his feelings and aims. He needs to stop pursuing his current policies, which do not enable him to achieve his goals, and he needs to return to the fundamentals. Since only a cultivated man (a gentleman) can maintain his constant moral feelings (*hengxin*) without having steady work (*hengchan*), the ruler must provide the conditions that will enable the people to have steady work. That in turn will enable them to behave in a moral way and support him.

Other passages do not literally use the term *quan* but demonstrate it nonetheless. For instance, Mencius illustrates his views with the behavior of Confucius, who best embodied sagely behavior, Mencius' ideal form of masculinity (2A2, 5B1, 5B4). He says that Confucius served in office or retired from office based on what was appropriate in the situation. His actions contrasted to those of Bo Yi, Yi Yin, and Hui of Liuxia. Bo Yi would not serve a ruler he did not respect and so was considered pure, that is, too rigid. Yi Yin would serve any ruler and so was too lax. Hui of Liuxia held onto his moral position but was viewed as too accommodating to others. Only Confucius exhibited proper timing in his actions. Mencius compares the behavior of Confucius to a great ritual musical performance, the completion of which is likened to the full development of sagely behavior. Going beyond merely the strength of reaching the target, sagely behavior is further compared here to hitting the mark. Another example of *quan* is how Confucius is said to have departed from a state (7B17). He left it slowly when it was the state of his father and mother and fast when it was the state of others.

The conflicts mentioned above that require a choice between ritual or moral behavior and what one wants or needs involve situational weighing, and Mencius provides other similar examples. For instance, faced with a choice between eating and ritual propriety, or a choice between getting a wife by improper means or not getting a wife at all, he says that one needs to consider the broader conditions, or weigh the situation—consider what is heavy and light, in making a decision (6B1). In some cases, the moral choice is more important, while in other cases it is not. As above, the two examples here of actions possibly antagonistic to ritual behavior also are linked to women.

While situational weighing is applied to various kinds of masculine behavior and its contexts, these passages illustrate some of the ways in which this concept is directly or indirectly linked to women, one's spontaneous moral feelings, and the notion of timing. Thought and deliberation are clearly aspects of situational weighing, but Mencius does not see them as opposed to and separate from one's spontaneous moral feelings. However, it is critical to Mencius' position that *quan* have its source in one's feelings and their development into the virtues, rather than in purely intellectual calculations. Clearly, the broader context of moral virtues, social circumstances, and natural conditions is also relevant.

From the above discussion, we thus see how Mencius' conception of the heart, or spontaneous moral feelings, is at the center of the processes of appropriation and transformation that help to form the Mencian ideal of masculinity. This ideal is that of the sage, a figure who acts within a male sphere of behavior. We have also seen that much of the thinking here is based on metaphors that concern farming practices. Given the transcoding of farming and maternal practices, maternal practices and thinking are thus implicitly present here although they are not the topic of interest.

Chapter 9

Gender, a Continuing Issue

Implications

In this study I have discussed how maternal ideas and practices are woven into the Mencian philosophical discourse about masculinities. In sum, the Mencian concept of the ruler as father and mother of the people entails a transformation and inversion of the practices of filial piety, which in turn are a transformation of maternal practices. These latter practices are culturally assumed to be based in the spontaneous and natural feelings of compassion of mothers. By claiming that men have these and other inborn feelings too, Mencius argues for a cosmic grounding of the patriarchal social virtues that can be developed from these feelings. Awareness of the links to female behavior can be a source of shame, however, and so Mencius disguises those associations even as he draws on them to develop his ideas and to reassure men that there is no shame in this sagely form of male behavior.

Additional textual evidence that links women in a fundamental way with the kind of feelings represented by the Mencian four innate moral feelings is vast and beyond the scope of this study, but a few further ideas can be pointed out. In actuality, regardless of their source, feelings are interrelated and not so easily separated as in Mencian theory. The four beginnings each are complex ideas that only appear to be simple on the surface. Separately and together, they consist of interrelated notions that to a great extent have a source in the practices and feelings of women as mothers and wives. The practices of farming require some similar feelings and behavior and so reinforce these ideas. Since only women can give birth and breast-feed babies, there was no doubt that women (even if not all women) had these maternal related characteristics.

A significant point about the notion of gender is that it separates the cultural meaning of behavior from the sexual characteristics of a person. While some practices may more often be thought of as feminine than masculine behavior, or vice versa, those cultural associations can change. Moreover, seemingly similar actions performed by men and women are culturally interpreted in different ways, since men and women each perform actions in reference to their own arenas of behavior. This is what we see happening with Mencian thought and its concern with establishing a new ideal of male behavior. At the same time, it is important to recognize that *Mencius* and other early philosophical texts simply do not address notions of femininity in a philosophical way. The behavior of men is the concern.

The claim of an innate source of moral feelings is critical. It is assumed that a mother's love and subsequent practices toward her children are natural. Although they can be improved upon by teaching and learning, they are not only a matter of teaching and learning. They may perhaps be suppressed, but they cannot be radically changed. Since maternal practices (including compassion) are not a result of human society, they are true of animals as well as humans. Thus the mother and child relationship is not a (patriarchal) social relationship that is open to change. By basing the five relations in the heart, Mencius turns these patriarchal social relations into natural ones too, just like the mother and child relation.

In order to provide the patriarchal order with the same grounding as a mother's loving practices and as the mother and son relationship, it is necessary to show that the components of patriarchy, especially the five relations and the four virtues, derive from innate characteristics of men. Mencius therefore argues that the four feelings are natural in men too, and their development leads to the four virtues. The social process is made analogous to maternal processes, as well as to farming practices, and so the difference between what is social and what is natural becomes obscured. A thread running throughout the text is the implicit comparison (and conflation) of Mencian patriarchal ideas and practices to maternal ideas and practices in respect to the innateness of their source and the importance of their cultivation. The latter (maternal ideas and practices) are accepted without question. To establish that the former (patriarchal ideas and practices) are equivalently unquestionable, it is necessary to show they have the same kind of innate basis. Although this view is stated in the *Odes* (for instance, Mao 260), Mencius goes further by providing an extended argument for it.

The four virtues of society fundamentally concern the father and son relationship. If these virtues were not based on innate feelings, however, then other ways of behaving could possibly take their place. If that were to happen, the father and son relationship could also be altered or replaced. Alternative virtues might support other relations than that of father and son. The authority and reality of the entire patriarchal system could weaken if it were based on optional, not innate, characteristics of men. In contrast, the mother and son (or mother and child) relationship can never be severed because it was believed to be based on innate characteristics of the world, animals as well as humans.

The father and son relation thus may be understood as a transformation in the social-political world of the mother and child relation in the biological sphere. With the latter as a given, the task was to provide convincing evidence that the former was equally unassailable, that social relations were as fixed and as natural as biological. Drawing on tradition, Mencius achieved this aim by appropriating beliefs about the characteristics of mothers (and farming) that people accepted without question and then applying them outside the maternal context to the male political sphere.

The Masculine Audience

Why does it matter in today's world that I have insisted we recognize that *Mencius* was and is addressed to men, that it concerns conflicts about masculinities, and that it appropriates and transforms behavior considered feminine? Why not simply say, as many contemporary thinkers do, that *Mencius* is addressed to all men and all women, that it concerns the behavior of all people, and that, even if *Mencius* were initially addressed to men and concerned with masculine behavior, the gendered behavior of the past is not relevant to today? The answer is twofold. First, gender is woven into the concepts themselves. We cannot understand Mencian concepts fully without taking into consideration as many of their dimensions as possible. Secondly, the gender dimensions of *Mencius* matter today because the issues and problems of gender still exist, and they cannot be genuinely addressed unless they are genuinely acknowledged. One does not have to exert much effort to look beyond the rhetoric of contemporary political leaders to see that their behavior in actuality often resembles that of the inhumane rulers whom Mencius opposed.

Those who deny the continuing realities of the hierarchical valuation of gender differences and their destructive effects on people's lives speak from a position of privilege, not from the lived experience of those affected. Moral ideals are of course critical to have, but to blur the distinctions between ideals and everyday actualities does more harm than good. At the very least, the stance of denial and blurring blatantly contradicts what many people know to be true from their own experiences, it further marginalizes those who are not in elite positions of power, and it leads to distrust and cynicism. Political leaders of today still bring shame on men who do not behave in that masculine way formerly opposed by Mencius, publicly calling them "girly-men" and by publicly claiming, in an undisguised patronizing tone, that some virtues may be nice in one's personal and family life but they are not appropriate in the realm of politics and government. They claim that the political realm requires (a masculinity of) aggression, domination, use of force, and denial of the ultimate effectiveness of other types of behavior, such as kindness and cooperation.

Unfortunately, this latter claim is true, for behavior and its institutional contexts are not separable. They mutually construct each other. Thus, changing ruthless and aggressive forms of masculine behavior today would require changing current social-political institutions and systems, and changing such institutions and systems would require, in turn, changing individuals' behavior. Mencius argued for this position by advocating a different form of government that would have benevolent policies, a new type of ruler who would exhibit a sagely type of masculinity, and a familial type of relation between the ruler and the ruled that would genuinely accept the humanity of everyone.

While many kinds of actions are needed to effect change in the contemporary world, one of the most important steps to be taken is that those in power and leadership positions must change their behavior, and no longer exhibit a masculinity of force. They themselves must be convinced that aggression and killing will ultimately destroy everyone. Unless permanent war is their goal, they cannot achieve even domination over others much less peace, with the methods they are using. They will not be convinced, however, by teachings and arguments that they consider either false or not relevant to them.

And this is the problem if we interpret Mencian teachings as being addressed to an audience that included (and includes) everyone, both males and females. Many people today, as in the past, both men and women, strongly believe, or rather "know," that there are fundamental, inborn differences among people, and they value these differences highly. Although many also accept the goal of modifying certain natural tendencies, most do not want gender and other differences to be obliterated. Thus, Mencian ideas about inborn feelings and their development, if applicable to everyone, can be considered not only based on inaccurate knowledge and so false, but they can also not even be a goal to be desired. Those to whom the ideas should be extended can easily ignore them.

Mencius' arguments to convince men to develop a different, and sagely, type of masculinity are insulting and insensitive if applied to women, for his arguments emphasize that such behavior will not result in a man's being considered like a woman or his feeling shame. Mencian models were great political and military leaders, which are not what a mother or wife typically aspired to become or what others in society wanted women to become. Similar ideas apply today. For people to change their ideal of masculine behavior, they needed and need to know that the new ideal is not feminine. If Mencian ideas apply to everyone, however, then such ideas cannot help but have feminine traits, which are still considered weak in the political world of today. As a result, a teaching about behavior that claims to apply to everyone in the end can be heard by almost no one, especially those political leaders whose behavior is of the type that Mencius wants to change.

Awareness

Although I have claimed that ideas about female gendered traits and practices are a hidden, or somewhat hidden, dimension of Confucian-Mencian thinking, I do not claim that some, or perhaps even many, thinkers were not aware of this dimension. The metonymic character of many terms and concepts and the acceptance of the view that ideas and events can have both surface and hidden meanings suggest that understanding the world through links of associations was widely accepted by Chinese thinkers. For example, interpreters of the *Spring and Autumn Annals* believed that particular terms express and conceal certain judgments, and many Daoist symbols have at the same time both alchemical and religious meanings. That Mencius actually addresses the issue of shame does suggest his and others' awareness to some extent.

Similarly, Mencius makes the claim that he understands words. He illustrates what he means by noting, for instance, that from biased words he knows how the speaker is deluded and from obscene words he knows how the speaker is entrapped. Mencius knows that words may literally express one idea while also having other meanings that a less perceptive person may not perceive. This kind of understanding is important because many practices originate in feelings, which often elude full verbalization or conceptualization.

In addition, the philosophical, cultural, and religious importance of mothers and the mother and son relation became increasingly explicit over time. In ancient China the way of the *ru* (Confucians) was compared to the maternal care of children. The later editions of the *Biographies of Famous Women* show an increasing emphasis on the moral virtues, as distinct from other abilities, of women, and all versions have many stories about mothers and sons.[1] By the late Ming, the concept of the way of mother and son was widely popular, at least among the elite.

By referring to later historical developments I am not claiming that these developments were inevitable. Rather, what I am suggesting is that we often do not see the imperceptible beginnings and nonobvious signs of phenomena and we only acknowledge the phenomena after they become obvious. Often, values and ideas that support certain kinds of behavior can be found in some form in the classical texts, but these values and ideas remain unnoticed as long as that behavior is not a matter of interest or not developed. Historical circumstances may be such that certain patterns of behavior never develop or never become noteworthy even though they do exist. A combination of circumstances may, however, lead to their becoming important. Even then, the earlier texts' expression of the values may not be relevant to their later development.

However, in the case of *Mencius*, we find that this text was an important philosophical source from the Tang period on. Its ideas were critical to many of the contested issues from the Song to the Qing, and many philosophers of this period knowingly quoted it in their own works. Thus I see this text as one that philosophers recognized and used as providing a continuing affirmation of many values, and so it did have a role in the historical development of certain patterns of behavior. The fact that maternal values can be found in *Mencius* does not at all mean, however, that their later valuation was inevitable or that they were not valued just as much in earlier times.

Whatever the extent of past thinkers' awareness of the maternal dimension in Confucian-Mencian thinking, I maintain that it is important to recognize it now. Such recognition would lead to a more sophisticated understanding of Chinese philosophy, culture, and history, and it would acknowledge the presence of certain perspectives that have historically been marginalized, suppressed, or simply not seen. In terms of historical understanding, a recognition that certain ideas and values were implicitly based on maternal thinking and practices would contribute to our further understanding of how women and men were able to support Confucian-Mencian thought despite its oppressive features and how this tradition was able to survive for many centuries.

In regard to historically unvoiced perspectives, such recognition would speak to a variety of contemporary issues and offer a contribution to the cross-cultural study of women and men, gender, and comparative philosophy. The recognition of a maternal dimension suggests that women were intellectually important to the philosophical tradition, even though acknowledgment of that importance was certainly limited. Perhaps even more significant, such recognition would provide further insight into cultural processes of transgendering. Transgendering is characteristic of many cultures, and it takes many forms. Although its meanings vary, one is that it signifies an attempt to overcome cultural binary categories, which are restrictive by their very nature. In Chinese religion, for example, the bodhisattva Guanyin provides a leading example of this process, while in literature Baoyu, the protagonist in *Dream of the Red Chamber*, is comparably outstanding. Indeed, there is strong indication that all the major philosophical and religious traditions of the world embody transgendering processes.

Within Confucianism, *Mencius* provides an outstanding illustration of both the pervasiveness of transgendering and how the processes worked. A reading of the text from this perspective will likely reveal aspects of this thinking that were heretofore hidden in plain view. It may also help contemporary people address the continuing problems associated with inhumane behavior. Ideas in addition to those discussed here are bound to emerge if we read this and other texts as cultural landscapes with many of their features still unknown and unexplored. Such exploration will depend, I suspect, upon how courageous we are in insisting that we imagine beyond the confines of cultural boundaries.

Notes

Chapter One

1. The distinction between gender and sex is a contemporary Western construct, and prior to modern times a person's behavior (gender) was typically not distinguished from a person's anatomy (sex). To reflect traditional Chinese views, I use the terms male and masculine, and female and feminine, interchangeably. For further discussion, see Brownell and Wasserstrom, 24–26; Laqueur; and Furth. Delphy, 63–76, claims that the sex/gender distinction of twentieth-century scholarship should specifically be credited to Margaret Mead, who first used it in her *Sex and Temperament*, and to Simone de Beauvoir and others who subsequently developed the ideas.

2. Scholars are increasingly incorporating the newly recovered texts and their ideas in their studies. To cite only a few examples, see Csikszentmihalyi; Yates; Ames and Hall, *Focusing*; Ames and Hall, *Daodejing*; and Behuniak, Jr.

3. *Lunyu* (*Analects*) 8.20. Some scholars interpret this passage as having a favorable view of women. For two of the many translations available, see Lau, *Confucius, The Analects*; and Ames and Henry Rosemont, Jr.

4. Many Western philosophers and scholars have pursued a similar approach, widely seen as stimulated by Nietzsche, whose numerous comments about women and woman include: "Suppose truth is a woman—what then?" and "Yes, life is a woman!" See respectively Nietzsche, *Beyond Good and Evil*, 1, and Nietzsche, *The Gay Science*, sec. 339, 193.

5. To reference Nietzsche again and Peter J. Burgard's claim, "He [Nietzsche] includes woman, accords the feminine a central role, in the articulation of his philosophy, even as his extreme sexism excludes woman." See Burgard, "Introduction," 12. Commenting on Nietzsche, Inglis and Steinfeld suggest that in criticizing the morality of Christianity as the virtues of women and slaves, and in contrasting it to a Roman, heroic, masculine morality, Nietzsche was in effect acknowledging transgendering processes in morality while also denigrating women. See Inglis and Steinfeld, 131–167. Other traditions of philosophical and religious thinking are beyond the scope of this analysis, but I suggest that the female may also implicitly be central to most if not all of them.

6. For current examples, see Brownell and Wasserstrom. Also consider the implications of the question they ask in the Afterword to their recent volume: "What if, instead of using history to explain gender, it [a book] used gender to explain history?" 435.

7. In preparing this study, I have consulted various editions of *Mencius* (*Mengzi*) in Chinese and English, including Legge, *Mencius*; Lau, *Mencius*; and *Mengzi xinyi* 孟子新譯 (A New Translation of Mencius), comp. Xie Bingying, et al. Throughout this study I have

checked my translations against those of Legge and Lau and have often used modifications of their translations. All references to Lau's translations are to his English only text. The analysis regarding gender in *Mencius* is my own, however.

8. Han Yu (768–824) is traditionally regarded as the thinker responsible for elevating the importance of *Mencius* for later thinkers with his idea of the *daotong* 道統 (orthodox transmission of the Way). See Wilson, *Genealogy*.

9. The list is long and still growing, but some major studies include Behuniak; Csikszentmihalyi; Shun; Nivison; Jullien; Ames, "Mencian Conception;" Chan; Huang, *Mencian Hermeneutics*; and Richards. Nivison discusses the backgrounds of some major translators of *Mencius* in *Ways*, 175–77.

10. For a discussion on the different perspectives that Chinese thinkers used for reading, see Wilson, "Messenger;" and Gu. For an overview of Chinese commentaries on *Mencius*, see Huang, *Mencian Hermeneutics*; and for examples of different contemporary readings of classical texts, see Yu, et al.; and Geaney, "Mencius's Hermeneutics."

11. Brooks and Brooks, "The Nature and Historical Context." See p. 273 for the dates of the added material in diagram form. The traditional dates for Mencius are 371 BCE–289 BCE, but Qian Mu has suggested 390 BCE–305 BCE, while the Brooks believe these dates are still uncertain. See Chan, 3, and Brooks and Brooks, 276, note 13. All the early texts were compiled over time by more than one person, and so this aspect of the textual history of *Mencius* is typical.

12. *Odes*, Mao 240. See Legge's commentary and translation, in Legge, *The She King*, 446–448; and Waley and Allen, 235–236.

13. See Eno; and Jensen.

14. For references to Zhu Xi and to mothers as teachers, and to Li Yong, see respectively Birge; and my *Li Yong*.

15. See my article, "Cultural Patterns;" Hsiung-ping Chen; Cole; and Brown.

16. Mann, *Precious Records*.

17. See, for example, *Xunzi* 20/29 "Way of the Son;" *Mencius* 1A7, 1B5, and 2A5; and *Lunyu* 13.18.

18. Among the numerous examples, see *Mencius* 3B2, 3B3, and 3B4; and *Mozi* 墨子 8/32 "Against Music."

19. As Delphy points out, the sex/gender distinction is problematic for feminists because it is a cultural distinction that perpetuates the male/female and other hierarchies in society. I would add that the same could be said for the *yinyang* distinction. That is, in whatever context *yinyang* is applied, the *yin* position is spatially lower and is implicitly associated with a "female" position. This view is prominent in the Daoist text *Daodejing* 道德經 (*Laozi* 老子) but came to be accepted throughout Chinese culture. See *Daodejing*, ch. 28, for an example of *yin* strategies' being advocated to achieve a *yang* goal of sagehood.

20. For example, Mao 260, in Waley and Allen, 275–277.

21. Geaney, "Guarding." Reference is to *Xunzi* 3/5 "Against Physiognomy."

22. Maram Epstein discusses this point in reference to late imperial fiction. See her *Competing Discourses*. Some scholars point to an origin of *yinyang* to which gender is irrelevant, a claim about which I have serious reservations, but in any case origin does not determine later social meanings and usage, which is the issue here. Also see Rouzer.

23. I use Iris Young's definition of the concept of oppression, as a grouping of social conditions experienced by social groups and summarized by this general term, oppression. See Young. Although her analysis examines such conditions as exclusion, denigration, exploitation, marginalization, powerlessness, violence, and cultural imperialism in American society, Chinese society exhibits many comparable conditions. The complexity of human experience is such that the recognition of oppression does not necessarily preclude the existence of certain opportunities, including learning to read, write, paint, or becoming honorary gentlemen. The fact that women or men themselves carried out certain practices, such as footbinding in the case of women, does not negate its oppressive aspects. For a discussion on how and why people come to discipline themselves, see Bartky.

24. The relationship between actual social conditions for women and what thinkers and texts said about women, the female, and the feminine, is complex. To cite just a few studies, see Nylan, "Golden Spindles;" Raphals, "Gendered Virtue;" Raphals, *Sharing the Light*; Bray; Ko; Mann and Cheng; and Wang.

25. For instance, in the *Odes*, Mao 192, Lady Bao Si, rather than the king, is blamed for the fall of the Western Zhou dynasty in 771 BCE because of her close relationship with King You.

26. *The New York Times*, May 5, 2002, p. 3.

27. Ellen Marie Chen.

28. See duBois; and Inglis and Steinfeld.

29. Respectively, Elvin and Liu, 2; Bray; and Epstein.

30. Lewis.

31. Geaney, "Feminine and Beastly Nature," 8. Reference is to *Xunzi* 13/19 "On Ritual." In English, breast-feeding is not necessary for feeding. The claim of the father's begetting the child but not nourishing/breast-feeding the child (*funengshengzhi, bunengyangzhi* 父能生之, 不能養之) offers an example of (long forgotten) appropriation and transformation, with *sheng* expanding to mean "to beget" as well as "to give birth."

32. The work of Western writers in this regard is voluminous. For two early and influential works, see Gilligan; and Ruddick.

Chapter Two

1. Although scholars often use the terms class and role in reference to Chinese society, these English words are not a translation of premodern Chinese words or concepts. Chinese philosophical texts refer to specific relations and to occupations or types, such as the four [types of] people (*simin*)—gentlemen or officials, farmers, artisans, and merchants. Scholars have long recognized that each class has social, economic, political,

and moral dimensions, but until recently they have not addressed the issue of, or acknowledged, a gender dimension. I use the terms class and role in a Confucian sense.

2. Numerous passages indicate that the text is addressed to men by the fact that only they can perform the actions in question, such as getting a wife (6B1) or behaving as a good son (1A3).

3. Since the type of claims I make about this passage is the subject of much discussion in the following chapters, I do not offer any extended support for them here. According to the Brooks' analysis, Book 7 belongs to the last northern layer of the text.

4. In 1A7, for instance, in a reference to the ruler's enabling the people (*min*) to have sufficient means of support, a man in the relational positions of son, father, and husband is the subject, and his father and mother, wife and children, are the recipients of his actions. In 1B5, criminals are assumed to be men, for the text says that their punishment does not also apply to their wives and children.

5. Listing of occupations and activities occurs in various passages, such as 1A7 and 1B5.

6. For instance, *zhuangzhe,* the able-bodied or strong [young men], in 1B12; *xuezhe,* [male] students, in 3B4; and *yingcai,* the talented young [men], in 7A20.

7. The major full translations are those of Legge, Lau, and Dobson.

8. *Xunzi* later emphasized these ideas, especially in the chapter on ritual.

9. A similar inclusive use occurs in 3A4 with *yirenzhishen* 一人之身, which Lau, *Mencius,* translates as "each man," 101. The passage then emphasizes the difference between the great men and the commoners.

10. Lau, *Mencius,* translates *ren* as human, however, thus masking the gender and class dimensions, 168.

11. Ruddick, 13–14.

12. Ibid., 24.

13. Numerous studies of transsexuality indicate that there is much more physiological variation in infants than the notion of two sexes implies. In one of the earlier references to this phenomenon, Ellen Kaschak points this out in her *Engendered Lives*, 38–42.

14. Adrienne Rich emphasizes this point in her *Of Woman Born*, 101.

15. Ruddick, 22.

16. In 3A5 (the last southern textual layer), Yizi comments that according to the Confucians the ancient rulers governed as if they were taking care of an infant. Both Yizi, a Mohist rival of Mencius, and Mencius ignore the indirect reference to maternal love and instead focus on the issue of gradations in love, i. e., loving family members versus others. Han Feizi, a slightly later Legalist thinker, also was critical of Confucian-Mencian thinkers who advocated governing compassionately as if the people were infants. See, for example, *Han Feizi* 19/50.

17. Ruddick, 24.

18. Nylan, "Han Classicists," 149.

Chapter Three

1. See Lau, *Mencius*, for a translation of 3A4, 100–105; or Legge, *Mencius*, 246–256. Legge's translation includes the Chinese text along with his translation into English.

2. For the latter contribution, see Smith, *Fortune-tellers*, 13.

3. See *Mencius* 2A6.

4. See *Odes*, Mao 236.

5. I borrow this phrase from Epstein.

6. See the Warring States Workshop online discussion, messages 814, 816, and 828, from Paul R. Golden, Martin Kern, and Whalen Lai respectively, at the following website: http://groups.yahoo.com/groups/wsw/.

7. *Fuziyouqin*, *junchenyouyi*, *fufuyoubie*, *zhangyouyouxu*, *pengyouyouxin* 父子有親, 君臣有義, 夫婦有別, 長幼有序, 朋友有信. The translations of both Legge and Lau clearly reflect that these ways of behaving are what should be taught to the people, since they do not already practice them.

8. The expansion to five is significant in terms of the gender dimension of the philosophical argument, as my discussion in chapter 8 will suggest. To compare, Mozi, who lived before Mencius, focuses on only two or three relations. For instance, *Mozi* 4/16 "Universal love" addresses the appropriate kinds of behavior between ruler and minister and between father and son; and *Mozi* 8/31 "Understanding ghosts" mentions the kinds of behavior between rulers and ministers, fathers and sons, and older brothers and younger brothers. It is clearly understood that certain kinds of behavior apply specifically to certain relations of males.

9. Mencius' contemporary Zhuangzi, from the southern region of Chu, also addresses this issue and sees likeness or sameness and difference as a matter of language in his *Qiwulun* (On making things the same) chapter in *Zhuangzi*. I find Lau's translation of *tong* as equal (and *buqi* as unequal) to be somewhat misleading in this context, *Mencius*, 104.

10. In 6A7 Mencius claims that men all are of the same category—*tonglei* 同類.

Chapter Four

1. I take *guoren* 國人 (stranger) here to be similar in construction to *xiangren* 鄉人 (villager) in 4B28 and to *minren* and *shengren* in 3A4. By interpreting *guoren* as similar to *luren* 路人 (following Zhu Xi) in meaning men on the road, travelers, or strangers, one can see that these are social categories: road type of men, village type of men, the people type of men, sages type of men.

2. The analogy between music and social relations was important for most Chinese thinkers and Mencius is no exception. One example occurs in 1B4, in which Duke Jing asks the Grand Musician to play music for him that expresses the mutual pleasure between ruler and minister. Also see 2A2, which links a ruler's ritual practices and musical performances to the morality of his government and himself.

3. His supposed commoner status is usually derived from his being found in the fields and so the claim was that he was a commoner. Given what we know about ancient China, many scholars question this literal interpretation and have suggested a variety of other interpretations, including escape from his evil stepmother.

4. Yang Zhu and Mo Di embody other transformations of these two rejected forms of masculinity represented here by Shen Nong and King Hui of Liang.

5. Benevolence and rightness (*renyi*) are found throughout the text, including the original Mencius interviews; kindness (*en*), protecting and nurturing (*bao*), treating old and young appropriately (*laowulao, youwuyou*), maintaining unwavering moral feelings (*hengxin*), and holding on to the fundamentals (*ben*) all appear in the later layers, for example, 1A7, the fifth layer. Practicing respectfulness, thriftiness, courtesy, and humility (*gong, jian, li, xia*) also appear later, in 3A3, the last southern or seventh layer.

6. The meanings of *ren* and *yi* are a topic of discussion in chapter 6 below.

7. Reflecting the importance of relations, the injunctions are: first, punish unfilial sons, do not disinherit heirs, and do not elevate concubines to wife; second, honor virtuous men and train talented men and thereby make the virtuous known; third, respect the old and be kind to the young, and do not forget guests and travelers; fourth, do not let gentlemen hold hereditary office, let men hold only one office at a time, select gentlemen appropriately, and do not execute an official without consulting others; fifth, do not divert dikes, do not prohibit the sale of rice to other states, and report all fiefs that are granted (6B7).

CHAPTER FIVE

1. Mencian views on benevolence and rightness are discussed here only in terms of governmental practices; their relation to the king's personal behavior will be addressed in the following chapters. I recognize that the translation of such key philosophical terms as *ren* (translated here as benevolence) and *yi* (translated here as rightness or dutifulness) is now a matter of much scholarly interest and dispute, but discussion of this issue is beyond the scope of this study.

2. This and related concepts are discussed further in chapter 6.

3. Mentioned previously, this important image is discussed further in chapter 7.

4. The idea of planning ahead contrasts to Zhuangzi's contemporary idea of naturalness or spontaneity, which characterizes the way of nature as opposed to human society.

5. The first four textual layers do not mention support of wife and children.

6. The wifely behavior of being respectful, thrifty, courteous, deferential, and restrained is discussed in the following chapters.

7. For an insightful discussion on Mencius and pleasure, see Nylan, with Huang, "Mencius on Pleasure."

8. Although *se* is often translated as sex or beauty, men are the subjects and women are the objects, for the assumption is that men are the ones who have sex with women. Another passage, 6B1, explicitly uses the word *se* to refer to *qi*, wife. In other texts when men are both the subject and object in a sexual relation, the term used is *nanse* 男色 (male sex).

Chapter Six

1. Until relatively recently Western studies on the self routinely ignored issues of gender, class, and relationships, and they implicitly considered the self as an independent male subject. An example is Carrithers, et al.

2. For instance, Mencius says (in 7B9) that, if you yourself (a married male) do not practice *dao*, then it will not be practiced by your wife (and children).

3. I translate *chen* 臣 as either minister or vassal, depending on what seems more appropriate in a particular passage. When either translation is possible, I use minister.

4. I translate *zhe* as a man, rather than as one who, since the setting consists of men's activities.

5. Much later in history, the term *nüjunzi* 女君子 (female gentleman) appeared, thus openly indicating the male gendering of *junzi*.

6. For the relevance of this passage to the issue of shame, see chapter 8.

7. Note the similarity in message between this passage and the opening passage of the text (1A1), cited above.

Chapter Seven

1. Except for possibly 1A6 and the term water, the original interviews do not contain terms having obvious maternal associations.

2. Examples are found, for instance, in 1A1, 1A6, 1B16.

3. Here I take *qin* as father, not parents, because the following lines are about Shun's pleasing the blind man, his father, and there is nothing said here about his mother.

4. A similar passage occurs in the *Analects* 19.17, which dates from about 253 BCE according to the Brooks' analysis, close to the time of *Mencius* 3A2 (ca. 254–249 BCE) and long after Mencius' death in about 303 BCE.

5. I translate *qin* as father, not as parents, since the conversation in this passage is clearly about governmental matters and elite men in a political context. When the deceased person is one's mother, that fact is made explicit. For instance, in 7A39, Mencius takes up the matter of whether a man can cut short the required period of mourning. Mencius says that it is best to teach a man the duties of being a good son and younger brother, but in a case like that of the prince, whose mother died, a man can cut short the period of mourning if it is necessary. This passage is identical to that in the *Analects* 2.5, which dates from about 317 BCE, during the period of the original Mencius interviews, ca. 320–310 BCE.

6. Further examples are found in 1A7, 5A5, 5B7, and 7B31.

7. In chapter 8, I discuss shame, the four beginnings, and the maternal heart.

Chapter Eight

1. For issues regarding *xing*, see Ames, "The Mencian Conception," Shun, Behuniak, and Bloom.

2. Although not the only number of categorization, groupings of four include such diverse things as the four limbs (of the body), the four social classes, the four virtues, and the four seasons.

3. See Geaney, "Guarding." Since Geaney discusses Chinese and Western scholarly views on shame in this article, I do not repeat the arguments and sources here. However, her article and the ones that she cites do not discuss how shame is closely related to gender issues and how shame differs for men and women.

4. See Louie and Edwards,

5. According to Legge, *Mencius* 2A2, 187, note.

6. Note the use of *hao* (flood-like) in the *Shujing* (classic of *Documents*), where *hao* refers to Yao's flood, so vast, overflowing, and uncontrollable, thus causing great suffering. See, for instance, Legge, *The Shoo King*, "The Canon of Yao," 24, and "Yi and Ji," 77.

7. See Legge, *The She King*, 544; and Waley and Allen, 276.

8. In 7A.14 it is claimed that a benevolent reputation is more important than just benevolent words. The point is that one's actions count more than one's words.

9. *Xing* and *cai* may or may not refer to feelings, for there are other kinds of natural tendencies and abilities. *Qing* may include other feelings in addition to those identified as the four beginnings of morality and has meanings other than feelings in other contexts. Suggesting developments in philosophical discourse, these terms do not appear in the earliest layers of the text. *Xing* (natural tendencies) only appears in the last two layers (chapters 6, 7, and 3), *qing* (feelings) only appears here in this sense, and *cai* (natural abilities) also appears only in later passages (for instance, 1B7, 6A6–7, and 7B29).

10. See Legge, *The She King*, 541; and Waley and Allen, 275.

11. Legge says "normal virtue," 541; Waley and Allen "seemly behavior," 275; and Lau, *Mencius*, "superior virtue," 163.

12. *Li* is also a term that does not appear in the early layers of the text.

13. This passage uses four terms—*xing*, *qing*, *liangxin*, and *renyizhixin*, to refer to the heart's natural moral feelings, making these four terms synonyms in this sense. I list them here in order from the most abstract to the most specific. Although the specific application is not apparent in the more abstract terms, it still remains, implicitly understood.

CHAPTER NINE

1. See discussion by Raphals, *Sharing the Light*.

Bibliography

Ames, Roger T. "The Mencian Conception of *Renxing*: Does it Mean 'Human Nature'?" In *Chinese Texts and Philosophical Contexts: Essays Dedicated to Angus C. Graham*, edited by Henry Rosemont, Jr., 143–75. LaSalle, IL: Open Court, 1991.

Ames, Roger T., and David L. Hall. *Focusing the Familiar: A Translation and Philosophical Interpretation of the Zhongyong*. Honolulu: University of Hawaii Press, 2001.

———. *Daodejing: "Making This Life Significant" A Philosophical Translation*. New York: Ballantine Books, 2003.

Ames, Roger T., and Henry Rosemont, Jr. *The Analects of Confucius: A Philosophical Translation*. New York: Ballantine Books, 1998.

Barlow, Tani. "Introduction." In *Gender Politics in Modern China: Writing and Feminism*, edited by T. Barlow, 1–12. Durham, NC: Duke University Press, 1993.

Barlow, Tani. "Theorizing Women: *Funü, Guojia, Jiating*." In *Body, Subject, and Power in China*, edited by Angela Zito and Tani Barlow, 253–89. Chicago: University of Chicago Press, 1994.

Bartky, Sandra Lee. "Foucault, Femininity and the Modernization of Patriarchal Power." In *Feminism and Foucault: Reflections on Resistance*, edited by Irene Diamond and Lee Quinby, 61–86. Boston: Northeastern University Press, 1988.

Behuniak, James, Jr. *Mencius on Becoming Human*. Albany: State University of New York Press, 2005.

Birdwhistell, Anne (Joanne) D. "Cultural Patterns and the Way of Mother and Son: An Early Qing Case." *Philosophy East and West* 42 no. 3 (July 1992): 503–16.

———. *Li Yong (1627–1705) and Epistemological Dimensions of Confucian Philosophy*. Stanford, CA: Stanford University Press, 1996.

———. *Transition to Neo-Confucianism: Shao Yung on Knowledge and Symbols of Reality*. Stanford, CA: Stanford University Press, 1989.

Birge, Bettine. "Chu Hsi and Women's Education." In *Neo-Confucian Education: The Formative Stage*, edited by Wm. Theodore de Bary and John W. Chaffee, 325–67. Berkeley: University of California Press, 1989.

Bloom, Irene. "Biology and Culture in the Mencian View of Human Nature." In *Mencius: Contexts and Interpretations*, edited by Alan K. L. Chan, 91–102. Honolulu: University of Hawaii Press, 2002.

Bray, Francesca. *Technology and Gender: Fabrics of Power in Late Imperial China*. Berkeley: University of California Press, 1997.

Brooks, E. Bruce, and A. Taeko Brooks. *The Original Analects: Sayings of Confucius and His Successors*. New York: Columbia University Press, 1998.

———. "The Nature and Historical Context of the *Mencius*." In *Mencius: Contexts and Interpretations*, edited by Alan K. L. Chan, 242–81. Honolulu: University of Hawaii Press, 2002.

Brown, Miranda. "Sons and Mothers in Warring States and Han China, 453 BCE–220 CE." *Nan Nü* 5 no. 2 (2003): 137–69.

Brownell, Susan, and Jeffrey N. Wasserstrom, eds. *Chinese Femininities/Chinese Masculinities: A Reader*. Berkeley: University of California Press, 2002.

Burgard, Peter J. "Introduction: Figures of Excess." In *Nietzsche and the Feminine*, edited by Peter J. Burgard, 1–32. Charlottesville and London: University Press of Virginia, 1994.

———, ed. *Nietzsche and the Feminine*. Charlottesville and London: University Press of Virginia, 1994.

Carrithers, Michael, Steven Collins, and Steven Lukes. *The Category of the Person: Anthropology, Philosophy, History*. Cambridge: Cambridge University Press, 1985.

Chan, Alan K. L., ed. *Mencius: Contexts and Interpretations*. Honolulu: University of Hawaii Press, 2002.

Chandler, Marthe, and Ronnie Littlejohn, eds. *Polishing the Chinese Mirror: Essays in Honor of Henry Rosemont*. La Salle, IL: Open Court, 2006.

Chen, Ellen Marie. "Tao as the Great Mother and the Influence of Motherly Love in the Shaping of Chinese Philosophy." *History of Religions* 14 no. 1 (1974): 51–63.

Chen, Hsiung-ping. "Constructed Emotions: The Bond between Mothers and Sons in Late Imperial China." *Late Imperial China* 15 no. 1 (June 1994): 87–117.

Ching, Julia. "Sung Philosophers on Women." *Monumenta Serica* XLII (1994): 259–74.

Chung, Priscilla Ching. *Palace Women in the Northern Sung, 960–1126*. Leiden: E. J. Brill, 1981.

Cole, Alan. *Mothers and Sons in Chinese Buddhism*. Stanford, CA: Stanford University Press, 1998.

Csikszentmihalyi, Mark. *Material Virtue: Ethics and the Body in Early China*. Leiden and Boston: Brill, 2004.

de Bary, Wm. Theodore, and John W. Chaffee, eds. *Neo-Confucian Education: The Formative Stage*. Berkeley: University of California Press, 1989.

de Beauvoir, Simone. *The Second Sex*. Translated by H. M. Parshley. New York: Knopf, 1952. [*Le Deuxieme Sexe*. 2 vols. Paris: Gallimard, 1949].

Delphy, Christine. "Rethinking Sex and Gender." In *French Feminism Reader*, edited by Kelly Oliver, 63–76. Lanham, MD: Rowman and Littlefield, 2000.

Diamond, Irene, and Lee Quinby, eds. *Feminism and Foucault: Reflections on Resistance*. Boston: Northeastern University Press, 1988.

Dobson, W. A. C. H. *Mencius*. Toronto: University of Toronto Press, 1963.

duBois, Page. *Sowing the Body: Psychoanalysis and Ancient Representations of Women*. Chicago: University of Chicago Press, 1988.

Ebrey, Patricia Buckley. *The Inner Quarters: Marriage and the Lives of Chinese Women in the Sung Period*. Berkeley: University of California Press, 1993.

Elvin, Mark, and Liu Ts'ui-jung, eds. *Sediments of Time: Environment and Society in Chinese History*. Cambridge: Cambridge University Press, 1998.

Eno, Robert. "The Background of the Kong Family of Lu and the Origins of Ruism." *Early China* 28 (2003): 1–41.

Epstein, Maram. *Competing Discourses: Orthodoxy, Authenticity and Engendered Meanings in Late Imperial Chinese Fiction*. Cambridge, MA: Harvard University Press, 2001.

Furth, Charlotte. *A Flourishing Yin: Gender in China's Medical History, 960–1665*. Berkeley: University of California Press, 1999.

———. "Androgynous Males and Deficient Females: Biology and Gender Boundaries in Sixteenth- and Seventeenth-Century China." *Late Imperial China* 9 no. 2 (December 1988): 1–31.

Geaney, Jane. "Guarding Moral Boundaries: Shame in Early Confucianism." *Philosophy East and West* 54 no. 2 (April 2004): 113–42.

———. "Mencius's Hermeneutics." *Journal of Chinese Philosophy* 27 no. 1 (March 2000): 93–100.

———. "The Feminine and Beastly Nature of Filial Feeding." Paper presented at the annual meeting of the Association for Asian Studies, March 28, 2003.

Gilligan, Carol. *In a Different Voice: Psychological Theory and Women's Development*. Cambridge, MA: Harvard University Press, 1982.

Golden, Paul Rakita. "The View of Women in Early Confucianism." In *The Sage and the Second Sex: Confucianism, Ethics, and Gender*, edited by Chenyang Li, 133–61. LaSalle, IL: Open Court, 2000.

Gu, Ming Dong. *Chinese Theories of Reading and Writing: A Route to Hermeneutics and Open Poetics*. Albany: State University of New York Press, 2005.

Huang, Chün-chieh. *Mencian Hermeneutics: A History of Interpretations in China*. New Brunswick, NJ: Transaction Publishers, 2001.

———. *Mengzi*. Taipei: Sanmin shuju, 1993.

———. *Mengzi sixiang de lishi fazhan* [The Historical Development of Mencius' Thought]. Taipei: Zhongguo yanjiuyuan Zhongguo wenzhe yanjiusuo, 1995.

Inglis, Laura Lyn, and Peter K. Steinfeld. *Old Dead White Men's Philosophy*. Amherst, NY: Humanity Books, 2000.

Jensen, Lionel M. "Wise Man of the Wilds: Fatherlessness, Fertility, and the Mythic Exemplar, Kongzi." *Early China* 20 (1995): 407–37.

Jullien, Francois. *Fonder la Morale: Dialogue de Mencius avec un philosophe des Lumieres.* Paris: B. Grasset, 1995.

Kaschak, Ellen. *Engendered Lives: A New Psychology of Women's Experience.* New York: BasicBooks, 1992.

Ko, Dorothy. *Teachers of the Inner Chambers: Women and Culture in China, 1573–1722.* Stanford, CA: Stanford University Press, 1994.

Laqueur, Thomas. *Making Sex: Body and Gender from the Greeks to Freud.* Cambridge, MA: Harvard University Press, 1990.

Lau, D. C., trans. *Confucius, The Analects.* New York: Penguin Books, 1979.

———. *Mencius.* New York: Penguin Books, 1970; bilingual rev. ed. Hongkong: Chinese University of Hong Kong Press, 1984.

Legge, James, trans. *The Chinese Classics.* 5 vols. Vol. 2: *The Works of Mencius*; vol. 3: *The Shoo King*; vol. 4: *The She King.* Hongkong: The University of Hongkong Press, 1960.

Lewis, Mark Edward. *Writing and Authority in Early China.* Albany: SUNY Press, 1999.

Li, Chenyang, ed. *The Sage and the Second Sex: Confucianism, Ethics, and Gender.* La Salle, IL: Open Court, 2000.

Li Xiaojiang. "With What Discourse Do We Reflect on Chinese Women? Thoughts on Transnational Feminism in China." In *Spaces of Their Own: Women's Public Sphere in Transnational China*, edited by Mayfair Mei-hui Yang, 261–77. Minneapolis: University of Minnesota Press, 1999.

Louie, Kam, and Louise Edwards. "Chinese Masculinity: Theorizing *Wen* and *Wu*." *East Asian History* 8 (1994): 135–48.

Mann, Susan. *Precious Records: Women in China's Long Eighteenth Century.* Stanford, CA: Stanford University Press, 1997.

——— and Yu-yin Cheng, eds. *Under Confucian Eyes: Writings on Gender in Chinese History.* Berkeley: University of California Press, 2001.

McMahon, R. Keith. *Misers, Shrews, and Polygamists: Sexuality and Male-Female Relations in Eighteenth-Century Chinese Fiction.* Durham, NC: Duke University Press, 1995.

Mead, Margaret. *Sex and Temperament in Three Primitive Societies.* New York: William Morrow, 1935.

Mengzi xinyi 孟子新譯 (A New Translation of Mencius) in *Sishu xinyi* 四書新譯 (New Translations of the Four Books). Comp. Xie Bingying, et al. Taipei: Sanmin shuju, 1966.

Nietzsche, Friedrich. *Beyond Good and Evil: Prelude to a Philosophy of the Future.* Translated by Walter Kaufmann. New York: Vintage Books, rev. ed. 1989.

———. *The Gay Science.* Translated by Walter Kaufmann. New York: Random House, 1974.

Nivison, David S. *The Ways of Confucianism: Investigations in Chinese Philosophy.* Edited by Bryan W. Van Norden. Chicago and La Salle, IL: Open Court, 1996.

Nylan, Michael. "Golden Spindles and Axes: Elite Women in the Achaemenid and Han Empires." In *The Sage and the Second Sex: Confucianism, Ethics, and Gender*, edited by Chenyang Li, 199–222. La Salle, IL: Open Court, 2000.

———. "Han Classicists Writing in Dialogue about Their Own Tradition." *Philosophy East and West* 47 no. 2 (April 1997): 133–188.

Nylan, Michael with Harrison Huang. "Mencius on Pleasure." In *Polishing the Chinese Mirror: Essays in Honor of Henry Rosemont*, edited by Marthe Chandler and Ronnie Littlejohn, 1–26. La Salle, IL: Open Court, 2006.

O'Hara, Albert Richard. *The position of woman in early China according to the Lieh nü chuan, "The biographies of eminent Chinese women."* Washington, DC: The Catholic University of America Press, 1945.

Oliver, Kelly, ed. *French Feminism Reader*. Lanham, MD: Rowman and Littlefield, 2000.

On, Bat-Ami Bar, ed. *Engendering Origins: Critical Feminist Readings in Plato and Aristotle*. Albany: SUNY Press, 1994.

———. *Modern Engendering: Critical Feminist Readings in Modern Western Philosophy*. Albany: SUNY Press, 1994.

Raphals, Lisa. "Gendered Virtue Reconsidered: Notes from the Warring States and Han." In *The Sage and the Second Sex: Confucianism, Ethics, and Gender*, edited by Chenyang Li, 223–47. La Salle, IL: Open Court, 2000.

———. *Sharing the Light: Representations of Women and Virtue in Early China*. Albany: SUNY Press, 1998.

Rich, Adrienne. *Of Woman Born: Motherhood as Experience and Institution*. New York: Norton, 1976.

Richards, I. A. *Mencius on the Mind: Experiments in Multiple Definition*. London: Routledge & Kegan Paul, 1932.

Rosemont, Henry, Jr., ed. *Chinese Texts and Philosophical Contexts: Essays Dedicated to Angus C. Graham*. La Salle, IL: Open Court, 1991.

Rouzer, Paul. *Articulated Ladies: Gender and the Male Community in Early Chinese Texts*. Cambridge, MA: Harvard University Press, the Harvard University Asia Center for the Harvard-Yenching Institute, 2001.

Ruddick, Sara. *Maternal Thinking: Toward a Politics of Peace*. Boston: Beacon Press, 1989.

Shun, Kwong-loi. *Mencius and Early Chinese Thought*. Stanford, CA: Stanford University Press, 1997.

Smith, Richard J. *Fortune-tellers and Philosophers: Divination in Traditional Chinese Society*. Boulder, CO: Westview Press, 1991.

Sommer, Matthew. "Dangerous Males, Vulnerable Males, and Polluted Males: The Regulation of Masculinity in Qing Dynasty Law." In *Chinese Femininities/Chinese Masculinities: A Reader*, edited by Susan Brownell and Jeffrey N. Wasserstrom, 67–88. Berkeley: University of California Press, 2002.

The New York Times, May 5, 2002, p. 3.

Tu, Ching-I, ed. *Classics and Hermeneutics: The Hermeneutic Traditions in Chinese Culture.* New Brunswick, NJ: Transaction Publishers, 2000.

Waley, Arthur, trans., and Joseph R. Allen, ed. and trans. *The Book of Songs: Shijing. The Ancient Chinese Classic of Poetry.* NY: Grove Press, 1996.

Wang, Robin R., ed. *Images of Women in Chinese Thought and Culture: Writings from the Pre-Qin Period through the Song Dynasty.* Indianapolis: Hackett, 2003.

Wilson, Thomas A. *Genealogy of the Way: The Construction and Uses of the Confucian Tradition in Late Imperial China.* Stanford, CA: Stanford University Press, 1995.

———. "Messenger of the Ancient Sages: Song-Ming Confucian Hermeneutics of the Canonical and the Heretical." In *Classics and Hermeneutics: The Hermeneutic Traditions in Chinese Culture,* edited by Ching-I Tu, 107–25. New Brunswick, NJ: Transaction Publishers, 2000.

Yang, Mayfair Mei-hui, ed. *Spaces of Their Own: Women's Public Sphere in Transnational China.* Minneapolis: University of Minnesota Press, 1999.

Yates, Robin D. S., ed. *Five Lost Classics: Tao, Huanglao, and Yinyang in Han China.* NY: Random House, 1999.

Young, Iris Marion. *Justice and the Politics of Difference.* Princeton, NJ: Princeton University Press, 1990.

Xunzi jijie 荀子集解 (Collected Commentaries on *Xunzi*). Edited by Yang Jialuo. Taipei: Shijie shuju, 1966.

Yu, Pauline, Peter Bol, Willard Peterson, and Stephen Owen, eds. *Ways with Words: Writing about Reading Texts from Early China.* Berkeley: University of California Press, 2000.

Zhuangzi jishi 莊子集 釋 (Collected Commentaries on *Zhuangzi*). Edited by Yang Jialuo. Taipei: Shijie shuju, 1967.

Zito, Angela, and Tani Barlow, eds. *Body, Subject, and Power in China.* Chicago: University of Chicago Press, 1994.

Index